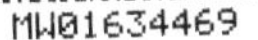

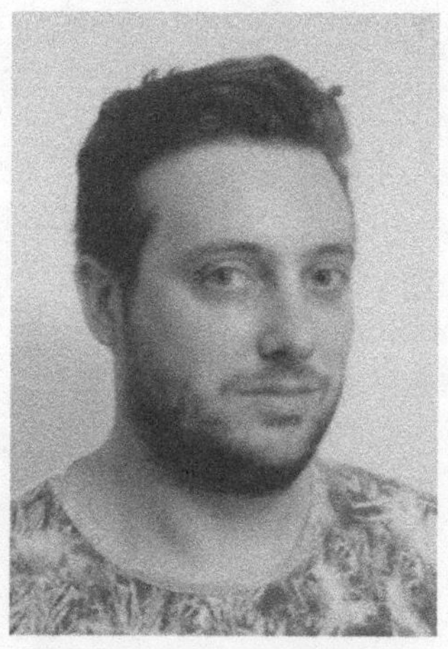

Brendan Shanahan is a writer based in Sydney and Las Vegas. He writes regularly for various publications internationally and is the author of *The Secret Life of the Gold Coast* (2004) and *In Turkey I am Beautiful* (2008). The latter was described as 'laugh out loud funny' by the *Sydney Morning Herald*, named 'one of the best travel books ever' by the *Sun Herald* and listed in the year's 10 best non-fiction works by ABC Radio National.

For Lee,
whose patience in the face of my self indulgence, poverty and
short attention span borders on saintly

A Note on Chronology

I have travelled, on and off, since the age of eighteen. This book is an attempt not only to chronicle some favourite anecdotes from those journeys, but also to justify what was a fairly lazy and debauched period. Because these stories cover a period of over ten years, starting in the mid–1990s, many details may now be out of date. Chinese television, for instance, has improved a lot but—from what I hear— the situation in some suburbs of Johannesburg has grown worse. I apologise if any of these obsolete details reflect poorly on a place or perpetuate redundant stereotypes— they were true at the time of writing, at least as I saw it. None of the journeys were commissioned or paid for by anyone but me. All are previously unpublished except 'Filler in Manila', which appeared (heavily edited) in the *Sunday Telegraph*'s *Sunday Magazine*. Some names and details have been changed.

MR SNACK

AND THE

LADY WATER

TRAVEL TALES FROM
MY LOST YEARS

BRENDAN SHANAHAN

MELBOURNE UNIVERSITY PRESS
An imprint of Melbourne University Publishing Limited
11–15 Argyle Place South, Carlton, Victoria 3053, Australia
mup-info@unimelb.edu.au
www.mup.com.au

First published 2013
Text © Brendan Shanahan 2013
Design and typography © Melbourne University Publishing Ltd 2013

Designed by Alice Graphics
Typeset by Typeskill
Printed in Australia by McPhersons Printing Group

National Library of Australia Cataloguing-in-Publication entry

Shanahan, Brendan, 1976-

Mr Snack and the ladywater / Brendan Shanahan.

9780522862232 (pbk.)
9780522862836 (ebook)

Shanahan, Brendan, 1976—Travel.
Voyages and travels—Anecdotes.

910.4

Contents

Mr Snack and the
Lady Water

Day 1

Until I arrived in China my interest in the Yangtze River and the famous stretch of it known as the Three Gorges was minimal. It was nevertheless a journey that lived in my imagination—a slow boat down the Yangtze had a certain ring of the familiar, if not of a novel I had read and forgotten, then a Sunday matinee seen one twilit afternoon, a technicolour fantasy starring Rita Hayworth dressed in a crimson cheongsam with her eyes taped back.

This newfound desire to travel down the Yangtze stemmed, in part, from the fact that the Chinese government was damming the great river to create the world's largest hydroelectric project. It was a process that would, ultimately, flood the Three Gorges, denying me and future generations the chance to see one of the world's great natural wonders, a source of inspiration to generations of Chinese writers and artists. I would normally have avoided any travel that might end in the line 'At least you can say you've seen it', but soon even that compensation would be denied me.

The overnight train from the western city of Xi'an had been unusually punishing. After an ill-conceived dinner of a tepid pork bun, most of the journey had been spent balancing over a rocking squat toilet in the posture of an unorthodox rodeo rider, doing my best to avoid the minefield of frozen phlegm wads scattered about my feet, glinting in the fluorescent light like massive emeralds.

Waiting for me in the dawn light at the station was a travel agent, an earnest young woman in a discordantly cheerful pink sweatshirt printed with a picture of Minnie Mouse. 'I take your bag,' she announced with the clipped efficiency that characterises much Chinese English. 'Tonight, you be at office. Five o'clock.' She pointed across the street. 'Don't be late,' she said, in a tone of menacing finality that might have proved useful at the entrance of say, an exclusive nightclub or concentration camp. And with that she marched off into the foggy street, my backpack in one hand, her sweater a pink ghost in the gathering grey.

The boats to the Three Gorges leave from the western river port of Chongqing, a vast industrial city in central China. According to the proud boasts of the city's tourist brochures, it was home to the country's largest aluminium factory and—more curiously—the world's biggest public toilet.

Despite ominous portents, Chongqing wasn't nearly as bad as expected. Here and there pockets of the old town remained. Street markets in the doorways of shabby homes offered ducks in bamboo cages or floppy carp in plastic buckets. The few surviving stepped alleys were relaxing oases free from the city traffic. From certain angles, the sorrowful blanket of mist that seemed to permanently shroud the skyline gave the city the look of a comic-book Gotham.

Any old-world appeal Chongqing may have possessed, however, was in the process of being vigorously scrubbed away. Construction sites covered the city; at every step signs appeared, cheerily announcing the imminent destruction of whole neighbourhoods. Huge malls stood eerily empty in the mist, props in China's coming capitalist surprise party. Soon only the world's biggest toilet would differentiate Chongqing from any other city in the country, a convenient metaphor for the future of China's urban life.

After a day of aimless wandering, I eventually made my way back to the travel agency. Inside, there was no sign of anyone except two elderly women perched on a bench by the door, engaged in a low, conspiratorial conversation.

Mandy and Tina were from Madison, Wisconsin, a fact they shared immediately, almost involuntarily, as if it were an extension of their names or an honorary title: 'Their Royal Highnesses Lady Mandy and Tina of Madison, Wisconsin.' It was but one of a number of, sometimes surprising, details of their lives I was to learn over the course of our journey.

'There's no one here,' said Tina to me, disapprovingly. 'Where is she? She said she'd be here. What if we miss the boat?'

'We could miss the boat,' said Mandy, staring anxiously about the room. 'It's not very professional.'

Over the next few days, Mandy and Tina were to become a subject of fascination to me. Although the pair had travelled extensively, including to a number of hazardous and obscure destinations, their adventures had inverted the usual effect of travel: instead of making them more confident and worldly, their globe-trekking seemed only to have exacerbated their anxieties and prejudices. Like elderly ninjas, every waking moment was spent in a state of alert. Their conversation was desperate and panicked, their movements excessively cautious, as if round every corner lurked scheming Oriental assassins covetous of their matching aquamarine backpacks and luminous white Reeboks.

Mandy and Tina's obsession with security was absolute; suspicion haunted every conversation and their luggage looked like a Houdini escape act, an Alcatraz of brass locks and cable wire sealing every pocket and zip. Even their make-up cases were armed with tiny combination locks, necessitating half an hour of intricate safe cracking every time they wanted to use a hairbrush. As they fussed with chains and inserted their passports into body cavities, I was struck by an image of their home: an enormous steel bank vault accessible only with dual keys and fingerprint recognition locks, the blast-proof circular doors opening slowly to offer them shelter from the freezing plains of Wisconsin.

Eventually, the tour guide arrived and announced our departure. Outside, a group of scrawny, desperate-looking porters descended on our luggage.

'No, no!' said Mandy. 'I can carry it myself!'

'We can carry!' cried Tina. 'Can carry! Can carry!'

Smiling as they ignored the women's pleas, the porters grabbed the bags, tied them to the yokes slung across their shoulders, and set off down the hill to the dock.

The dock was at the bottom of a steep embankment. An industrial elevator delivered us into the mass of passengers below. As we gathered our bags and made our way into the crowds, the porters—smiles replaced with grimaces of exhaustion—haggled over their payment.

'No! No!' said Tina in a dog-trainer tone as we reached the ticket barriers. 'Now, we were told that $1 was enough and this is all you can have.'

'Tina, stop arguing with them. Tell them it's enough.' Mandy turned to the porters and made exaggerated gestures of finality. 'Enough! Enough!' she said, karate chopping the air.

Down on the dock the crowds were milling about with the barely restrained belligerence of disaster evacuees. Shoulder to shoulder, thousands of people, many in matching baseball caps, shuffled in eddies about tired-looking women who waved little flags and screamed instructions into megaphones. Here and there passengers had arguments with relatives, or packed luggage into striped laundry bags the size of UN food drops, tying and retying them with nylon cord.

Moored to the dock was a large boat. Passengers streamed aboard over a rickety gangplank. It was older and shabbier than I had expected, with a hint of faded 1960s glamour. The foyer looked like an African dictator's airport hotel: chrome chandeliers, mirrored pillars and bronze horses galloping across the wall in high relief. As passengers streamed aboard the chandelier shook and jangled.

'I don't think this our ship,' said Mandy. 'Tina, ask her if this is our ship.'

With a revving of engines the water began to bubble and froth. In defensive huddles, the last passengers edged their way towards the gangplank, following the instructions of their tour guides.

'Excuse me,' I said, 'but shouldn't we be getting on board?'

'I'm pretty sure this is not our ship,' said Mandy confidently. She turned to the tour guide. 'This is not our ship, is it?'

'No,' said the tour guide. 'Not your ship.'

Mandy turned to Tina and made gestures of relief as the boat pulled away to reveal a dim form approaching in the dark.

The tour guide pointed. '*That* your ship.'

With mild horror I watched as the details came into focus. The hull was streaked with waterfalls of rust; the balconies stacked with old plastic chairs and cardboard boxes. Along the railings hung washing lines, rows of socks and several pairs of oversized white underpants flapping in the breeze. As the boat pulled in, hitting the dock with a thump, the hull shuddered and a cough of diesel smoke issued from the stack. A fine rain of soot showered our clothes and faces in a galaxy of tiny black stars.

'Oh, Tina, this can't be right,' said Mandy.

'Mandy, check the brochure. There must be some mistake!'

Mandy and Tina were not entirely alone in their distress. I'd be exaggerating if I said I had expected luxury, but neither had I been expecting something last seen taking Colonel Kurtz down river.

My booking had been made the previous week in Xi'an with a hotel manager and travel agent going by the alias Ronald McDonald. Grabbing me off the street and ushering me into his hotel, Ronald spread the brochures on the desk. Within their pages was a world of abundant luxury, the kind of middle-aged, breakfast-buffet comfort that seemed hopelessly out of my reach. 'Don't worry 'bout price,' said Ronald, waving his hand dismissively. 'You will see. Ronald McDonald will give you a happy deal. Huh, huh!' In retrospect, buying my ticket from a man masquerading as a hamburger chain mascot should have been a clear warning that this journey wasn't going to be everything I'd hoped.

With the arrival of the boat the crowd surged forward. The travel agent began to hand out boarding passes. 'There's been a mistake,' said Tina, fending off the shoving bodies. 'This is not like the brochure. Please, can you look at my ticket again?'

Ignoring her, the tour guide turned and handed me my boarding pass. 'Tell me,' I said, pointing to some Chinese characters on the rusted hull, 'is this the name of the boat?'

She nodded.

'What does it mean?'

She thought for a moment, brow furrowed with the effort of translation. 'It mean *Lady Water*,' she said, then sank back into the crowd, the route of her obviously well-rehearsed getaway marked by the occasional flashes of her pink sweatshirt amid the crowd.

Submitting myself to the crush of bodies, I was jostled along the rickety gangplank and deposited aboard the *Lady Water*. The interior equalled, if not surpassed, the shabbiness of the exterior. The foyer was an abandoned porn set. Sheets of wood veneer lining the walls buckled and curled from the damp. Vinyl couches riddled with cigarette burns hugged the corners. On one wall a gold picture frame hung empty, serving only to highlight the undulating veneer behind. Two large bronze plant-holders either side of the door struck the only note of glamour. Peering in I saw they were almost completely filled with cigarette butts.

The *Lady Water* had three passenger decks and a rooftop terrace. Connecting all levels was a wide spiral staircase, its walls lined with mirrors warped and discoloured by damp, multiplying passing passengers into an infinite refraction of carnival distortions as they climbed, bundles in hand, to their cabins. In the centre of the stairwell hung an enormous modernist chandelier. Its many golden arms supported only four functioning lights. With the engines revving the whole structure rattled, an ominous percussion that would be the soundtrack to my time aboard the *Lady Water*.

The hallways leading to the rooms were illuminated only by the eerie ambient light of the foyer and were carpeted in damp AstroTurf. With each cautious step it sprang back with a faint squelch.

'Oh, Mandy … Mandy,' chanted Tina as we made our way to our cabins, positioned across the hall from one another. 'This is just terrible.'

'Tina, do you think my hairdryer will work?'

I had decided to book a first-class cabin for my journey. This was an indulgence not normally possible on my budget, but one I had allowed myself after warnings from Ronald McDonald that anything less was likely to land me in a bunk-bedded purgatory of cigarette smoke, late-night karaoke and all-night spitting relays. As I slammed my shoulder into the swollen wooden door to my room I allowed myself the absurd hope that, by some chance, first-class would prove an oasis from the ship's dereliction.

With a final shove the door opened with a low harmonic twang. The room had the air of a by-the-hour motel, right down to the brown terry-towelling spreads on the twin beds and broken clock radio built into the side table. On each pillow lay a tiny towel, soap and a pair of white cotton slippers. The inclusion of these items, with their associations of cleanliness and luxury, seemed to me almost deliberately ironic as I inspected my surroundings. The walls and ceiling were pebble-dashed with mould. The bathroom was flooded in an inch of reeking, stagnant water; the bedroom carpet was the colour of pale mucus—appropriate considering it was speckled with a decade's worth of phlegm stains, spattered in a radiating pattern from the beds. The slippers took on a new significance.

Doing my best to mentally block out the filth, I banished the bedspread and began to unpack. My naive hope of a room to myself was dashed with the arrival of my roommate, a stocky Chinese man in grey slacks and an electric-blue vinyl jacket. I nodded and smiled hello. He responded with a brisk bow, his stony expression unchanged. Turning towards his bed he began to unpack with calm, studied gestures. From within his bags he produced dozens of food packages. Carefully, he lined up the chips, nuts and cookies on the side table then stacked the pot noodles in orderly, brightly coloured towers on the chair by the television. His task accomplished, he turned and sat down on the bed, pointing solemnly at the pile. 'Snarks,' he said, the only word of direct communication he was to offer me in the three days we would share a room.

Mr Snack's rations were a bad sign—bitter experience has taught me that when the locals bring their own food, you ignore their example at your peril. Through the window I could see a woman on the dock selling supplies. With only a short time before we left, I decided to take the opportunity to stock up.

On the deck I bargained for some overpriced pot noodles, cookies and a bony roast chicken. Returning with my haul I was surprised to find a young, attractive woman clutching a clipboard standing in the doorway in conversation with Mr Snack. Edging my way past, I greeted her. In response, she smiled broadly in a manner I found more menacing than reassuring.

'There is a problem,' she said, still smiling. 'I must have your bed.'

I sighed and dropped my chicken on the side table. Its head was still attached. Its eyes, burned black, stared out through the plastic. 'Why?'

'There is a mistake. Somebody else has booked this room. I am sorry.'

Producing my ticket, I made it clear that this was most definitely my room. The tour operator, however, was equally determined.

'I give you another room—better room!'

'Which?'

'Downstairs. With Europe boys. Your friends.'

She was referring, I presumed, to the pair of Irishmen I had met briefly on the dock. I was not overly excited by the proposition. They looked unkempt and fragrant, the sort given to drying their underpants on your bed railing and infecting your shower recess with fungal infections.

I thought for a moment. 'No,' I said and looked over at Mr Snack sitting on the edge of the bed, engrossed in a tourist brochure, judiciously ignoring our conversation. Her brow furrowed. 'Please,' she said, with a creeping desperation. 'I give you one hundred yuan.'

I said I didn't need it.

'Two hundred.' The bidding continued but I remained steadfast. 'Please,' she whimpered, pouting and cocking her head like a child. Mr Snack began to expectorate very loudly.

'I'm sorry,' I said. 'But I have been travelling for a long time and I would like this room so I can relax.'

'But they are your people!' she said accusingly.

I was tempted to explain that the Irish were almost as alien to me as the Chinese—and in light of several dangerous encounters in various pubs over the years, possibly more so—but decided instead to appropriate the ancient Oriental art of the stonewall.

At this point Mr Snack must have hit something really stubborn because he began to alternate his hawking with sharp, wet bursts of nasal exhalation, like a blue whale breaking the surface of the water.

'Six hundred,' she said and, for a moment, I considered accepting her offer: who knew which minor party official would be forced to sleep on the top bunk downstairs should she fail in her mission to evict me, and what horrible, petty revenge he would exact? This money, it occurred to me, was probably coming out of her own pocket, the threat of a transfer to Inner Mongolia still ringing in her ears. As it was, Mr Snack was ringing in mine and I began to wonder if her offer wasn't a blessing in disguise.

'You must leave,' she snapped. All at once the veneer of a congenial, put-upon underling slipped to reveal a ruthless operator who would as soon wave a busload of tourists into a re-education camp as show them the way to the toilets. Abruptly, Mr Snack finished making his sounds. With great dignity he leaned over the wastepaper bin and released a giant green teardrop. I watched as it slipped slowly from his lips, dangling momentarily on a silver web, before snapping off to hit the steel base of the bin with a thump.

Summoning all I had learned from the custodians of ticket booths and visa counters across Asia, I looked at the tour operator and slowly shook my head. She glared, and marched out of the room. Mr Snack, satisfied, curled up on his bed in his stockinged feet and opened one of his many packets. I watched him chew with an abstracted air, a self-conscious neutrality I found deeply suspicious.

A jolt, grinding gears and throbbing engines signalled the beginning of our journey. From the boat's roof deck I stood and watched ripples dissolve the neon in the water; the skyscrapers of Chongqing loomed silver in the dark. A small group had gathered to watch the view. As a passing cruise ship sent a slick of rainbow light onto the water, an old man on the deck burst into a melancholy song. It was a view I would come to look back on with a deep nostalgia, a sensation heightened no doubt, by the fact it was to be the only moment of happiness I was to experience aboard the *Lady Water*.

Steeling myself against the cold, I stood while the crowd dispersed and the lights of the city disappeared. Soon the smells of cooking rose from below. I looked at my itinerary. *Dinner: You will enjoy famous hotpot, most famous in all of Chongqing!*

The dining room of the *Lady Water* was to be guilty of many things, worst of all the instilling of false hope. Entering through swinging saloon doors one came upon a not-unpleasant room with the tarnished glamour of a suburban Chinese restaurant. To either side, under gilded chandeliers, people sat around three big circular tables. At their centres, lazy Susans spun merrily under the weight of plates of dumplings, steamed vegetables, bubbling pots of meat, noodles and even whole steamed fish. The atmosphere was convivial, full of raucous, getting-to-know-you laughter. As people ate they gesticulated with cigarettes and drank big bottles of beer.

It was a scene that would be repeated every mealtime aboard the *Lady Water*. Who these diners were however, and why they qualified for such sumptuous meals, would always remain a mystery, only deepened by the fact I was never to see these people outside this room.

At the back of the banquet room, through another set of swinging doors, was the main dining hall. To enter it was to be immediately transported to a scene of almost Dickensian bleakness. At dozens of plastic tables, diners sat among puddles of tea and a flotsam of cigarette butts, eating mush from steel cafeteria trays. From behind the counter, barrel-armed women ladled food from industrial cauldrons to the diners shuffling past in mute resignation. In here there were no loud conversations or laughter, no chandeliers or fragrant mounds of meat and fish, no sign of any hotpot, famous or otherwise. The sounds of chewing and the banging of steel trays were punctuated only by the occasional phlegm wad being hawked up and spat on the floor.

I approached one of the women behind the counter and gestured to the entry on my itinerary. 'Hotpot?' I said, full of hope. She looked at me, dropped her ladle into the cauldron and took a drag on her cigarette. I pointed towards the other room and made eating motions. With the entrance of each diner the sound of laughter echoed into the dining hall. She shrugged and pointed to the stack of prison trays. 'I will pay,' I said, rubbing imaginary bills between my fingers. With glazed eyes and an almost imperceptible shake of her head she pointed to the sign above the counter: *10 Yuan*. Stubbing out her cigarette into a tray of old food, she began to ladle piles of stew onto my tray.

Meals on the *Lady Water*, I was to discover, were not merely unappetising but lonely affairs. The Chinese passengers tended to move in tightly knit huddles, their dining tables as jealously guarded as a medieval hill fort. Any attempt to infiltrate was met only with blank stares, a stiffening of the shoulders and a subtle but pointed tucking in of chairs. It was obvious that, at mealtimes at least, I would have to content myself with the company of other foreigners. Unfortunately, aside from myself and Mandy and Tina, the only English speakers aboard the *Lady Water* were the two Irishmen. Everyone but us, it seemed, was determined we should be friends.

Liam and Fintan were, as it turned out, brothers, although they looked quite unalike. Fintan was blond with a Viking moustache and hawkish, starving features. Liam was dark with a boxer's nose. Both had quit their jobs to travel the world. For more than six months they had been on the road and would travel several more before settling in Australia to work.

For a while I made polite conversation. When I asked what they did for a living Fintan looked up and said, 'I'm a postman.' He paused before cocking his head. 'Do you have a problem with that?'

'Aw, don't mind him,' said Liam. 'He's just a grumpy bastard.' Fintan, ignoring his brother, stabbed at his food with a single chopstick held in his fist like a dagger. 'He's pissed off because he thought the tofu was chicken and ordered a double serving.' He leaned into his brother's face. 'You stupid thick cunt,' he said. 'Go on—eat up your fuckin' tofu. Eat it up.'

As his brother's mockery continued, the speed of Fintan's stabbing motion increased, the chopstick pounding a brutal Morse code on the steel stray.

'Whatsamatta? Don't like your tofu?'

Fintan dropped the chopstick into the middle of the tray. Slowly his head bowed, veiling his face in a tangle of blond hair. For a moment there was only the sound of the diners—the slurping, the spitting—and the increasing pace of Fintan's breathing. Without warning, he stood up, the scrape of his metal chair on the floor echoing loudly. There was a notable drop in volume among the diners. A couple at the next table looked up, rice bowls suspended before their faces. As the pause lengthened the hush grew, broken abruptly when, with one swift motion, Fintan grabbed a corner of the tray and, with all the casualness of a factory worker rejecting a rotten tomato from a conveyor belt, flipped it into the air.

The scene stays with me as if frozen in time: a rainbow wave of tofu, mushy greens and rice arcing across the table, the spiralling fingers of vegetable matter encouraging vaguely cosmological or aquatic associations—the early formations of a new galaxy or a ragged section of coral reef.

In a moment the spell was broken; gravity took over and the food hit the table with a wet *slap*. The clatter of the tray was kettledrums in the silence. Fintan turned on his heel and marched outside. The room was perfectly still, the eerie calm broken only by the swinging door and the slow percussive drip of tofu falling in thick drops from the table.

Almost as one, the gaze of the diners shifted from the door to us. 'Fuckin' grumpy cunt,' said Liam. He picked up his beer, leaving me to acknowledge the silent, staring faces with a fixed, apologetic grin.

Despite being arguably the loudest people on earth, the Chinese have an almost neurotic fear of conflict—fights are rare and great pains are taken to avoid them. *Luan*—chaos—is possibly the single biggest cultural taboo. As I sat staring out at all those blank faces, I was overwhelmed with the desire to protest my innocence. 'They're not with me!' I wanted to say. 'I just met them tonight. I don't even like the Irish!' But it wouldn't have made any difference: in their eyes I was just another big hairy westerner, a trouble-making, milk-drinking barbarian who, for the rest of this journey, would be a marked man, locked into a conspiracy with these Irish lunatics. The expression 'They all look the same to me' took on a new and painful irony.

With surprising speed the diners returned to their meals. The final notes of slurping and spitting soon sounded and, one by one, everyone began to file out the door. While I was still finishing, one of the barrel-armed canteen women appeared and began to clean up the tofu puddle on the floor. As she attacked it with a cloth I made sympathetic faces and gestured with my eyes at the remaining Irishman, like the victim of a kidnapping through the back window of a van. She just stared back silently, beams of hatred shooting from her pupils.

After finishing my meal I said goodnight to Liam and beat a hasty retreat to my room. Mr Snack was reclining on the bed in his socks and underpants, crunching rice crackers and watching a fuzzy documentary about river wetlands at heavy-metal volume.

Chinese television is diabolical. A typical evening might feature a rousing three-hour documentary detailing the duck-farming industry in the southern provinces, followed by a three-hour panel discussion on the topic, followed by a group of grinning schoolgirls in traditional dress performing a dismal music recital for a hall full of party officials in Mao suits and ballgowns. In Communist China, if religion was the opiate of the people, then television was the Thorazine.

Supplementing this relentlessly dreary diet was a seemingly never-ending stream of incomprehensible—albeit lively and richly wardrobed—historical soap operas. In structure these were much the same as their western counterparts, with the familiar quotient of illegitimate children, amnesiac resurrections and maternity mix-ups replaced with vicious martial-arts battles in which characters were beaten to death with clubs and infertility spells cast on their widows. These shows were a great favourite of Mr Snack. One in particular featured an evil local official who, in collusion with a trident-wielding fish spirit—and here I admit my understanding was conjectural—had impregnated a local princess with a form of demon child that she would be forced to make the inheritor of her estate and the custodian of a magic talisman with the power to make its wearer immortal. The program was vividly violent and the volume made it impossible to concentrate on anything else. As I sat and watched, Mr Snack turned and, with what I took to be a note of sympathy, silently offered a packet of spicy tofu chips.

After half an hour of television, consistent with what would prove to be his unfailing routine, Mr Snack folded back his covers, bowed goodnight, and climbed into bed. With his feet making a triangular peak at one end, he pulled the brown blankets to his chin and closed his eyes.

For a while I read by the light of the bedside lamp. Soon, however, I found my eyes growing heavy. Seduced by the silence, I turned out the light and lay in the dark. Slowly I grew aware of the sounds of the night: the rush of water by the window, the low hum of the engines, the rise and fall of Mr Snack's breathing. As I lay wrapped in my damp blankets, my mind began to calm, my tension to dissipate and, suddenly, the *Lady Water* didn't seem so bad.

While it was true it had fallen spectacularly short of its promise, I had endured worse, and who knew what morning would bring? After the shocks of the day it was easy to forget that I was still about to see one of the world's great natural wonders.

Soothed by these thoughts, I began to succumb to sleep. Not quickly enough, however, to insulate me from a series of unnerving sounds: the grinding of gears in an old car, a sock stuck in a vacuum cleaner, a whale breaking the surface of the ocean. On the other side of the nightstand, the silhouette of Mr Snack rose from the coffin of his bed. As the first wet slaps hit the bottom of the wastepaper bin I groaned, sandwiched my head in the mouldy pillow and, eventually, drifted off to the gentle surf of Mr Snack's expectoration.

Day 2

I usually avoid tour groups. The only thing I hate more than manufactured camaraderie is being told what to do. The idea that anyone might combine both and pay for the privilege is beyond my understanding. On the Yangtze cruise, however, it would seem I had no choice, a fact made very clear when at 3 a.m. there was an almighty thump on my cabin door.

Peeling open one eye I looked across the room to see a tour guide standing in the doorway, haloed by the bright light of the corridor. She was smiling with what I took to be a look of spiteful satisfaction. 'You wake up now,' she barked. I looked at Mr Snack, who was already slipping his yellow slacks over boxers the size of an Edwardian lady's bloomers. 'You go Chinese ghost city. You buy ticket.' She slammed the door and Mr Snack, now fully dressed, made a discreet bow and headed to the bathroom in little white slippers.

The sounds of phlegm being mined from deep nocturnal recesses soon filled the room. I rolled over and buried my fingers in my ears, at which point I became aware of a curious sensation. Below the waist, my body was almost completely numb. I began to panic. Sitting bolt upright I pounded my thighs with my fists and tried to kick my legs. With each punch, feeling returned and, as I lifted my legs out of bed and clomped my feet to the damp floor, blood prickled my limbs. With sensation returning, the slippery dampness of the phlegm-stained carpet sent chills of revulsion up my spine.

This was my first indication that our ship had a serious list. Looking about the room I noticed the water in the bottle on my nightstand was tipped at a twenty-degree angle. When I opened the window the curtains fell out. I looked over at Mr Snack's piles of food and was struck by the not entirely irrational thought that the only thing standing between us and capsizing was a single packet of soy chips. With some caution I climbed the hill to the door and made my way to the dining room.

Of all the bad meals I was to have on my Yangtze tour, breakfast was the best of a bad lot. Consisting of steamed buns stuffed with mystery meat and a bowl of flavour-less rice porridge, the first meal of the day had, at least, the consolation of being warm and filling. As the prison guards slopped the white goo into my bowl I scanned the room cautiously for the Irishmen. Thankfully, they were nowhere to be seen. At a table by themselves, Mandy and Tina were hunkered down over a meal of chocolate-chip cookies and tea.

'This is not good,' said Mandy as I joined them. 'This is really not good.'

'We're not happy,' said Tina. 'We're really not happy.'

I put my tray down and watched my teacup slide slowly to edge of the table. 'Aren't you eating the buns?' I asked.

'No way!' said Mandy.

'How would you know what they put in them?' said Tina. 'Did you hear they found a factory that was making children's toys with poison paints? What guarantee would you have that the same operation wasn't making those buns?

'We were promised a much better ship than this,' she continued. 'We were specifically told that we would have a sun deck, American breakfast and an English-speaking guide. But we don't even have a socket for the hairdryer!'

'If it was clean I wouldn't mind so much,' said Mandy. 'But my bed has mould on it. And our bathroom is this high with water.' She held up her forefinger and thumb.

'We got a pool alright,' said Mandy. 'A gosh-darn—excuse my language—a gosh-darn pool of stinky river water.' She took a breath and bit a cookie. 'I'm trying to find out how this happened, but no one will answer my questions.' As she spoke crumbs fell from the side of her mouth. 'If my husband had been here you can bet they'd have listened to *him*. But oh no, we're just a pair of dumb women. Well, I'm sick of it, absolutely sick of it. But don't you worry, they'll find out they can't do this to *us*.'

Since I had met them, the marital status of Mandy and Tina had been a matter of mild intrigue. This mention of a husband piqued my curiosity. If they were married, then why were they travelling together? Perhaps her use of past tense meant he was dead. Were they, I wondered, simply a pair of widows, out to see the world, or was there another, less expected explanation?

Through the mist the boat began to approach the shore. As if privy to secret information, the dining room rose as one and moved towards the exit.

In the foyer, a sea of matching baseball caps stretched to each wood-panelled wall, spread out onto the decks, snaked up the stairs and down the hallways. Punctuating the crowd, tour leaders with megaphones barked instructions at their groups, the feedback squalls and echoes of their monologues a painful avant-garde opera in the grey morning.

'Where are we going?' Tina cried over the din. 'What's happening?'

As the boat bumped into the dock the crowd pushed forward in anticipation. A sullen man outside the barrier, a cigarette clinging to his bottom lip, pulled back the gate. Stretching out over a shallow but swift-moving stream of mud, a wooden jetty floated on a series of precarious-looking pontoons. The crush of bodies propelled us towards the water. Beside me, Mandy and Tina were quickly swallowed up. 'Stop pushing!' they cried over the stomp of feet and the squall of the megaphones. 'What is the hurry?' The last I was to see of them that day was a pair of hands raised above the crowd in a futile gesture of entreaty.

As a nation of more than one billion, it often seems that the Chinese are so in the habit of pushing, shoving and fighting for everything that they tend to extend this behaviour to all situations, regardless of urgency—a tour of a historical site is met with the same sense of barely repressed hysteria as a bomb threat or hurricane evacuation. As ridiculous as it seemed, it was tempting to be caught up in the madness of the mob, as if this was a game show and the first person to the top of the mountain won a plasma TV or a holiday to Spain. Surrendering to the feverish crowd, I shoved my way onto the treacherous, mud-slicked gangplank and groped through the fog to shore.

The entrance to Fengdu was up a long zigzag embankment, soon to be flooded by the rising river waters. To reach it we had first to walk through a wasteland of abandoned apartment buildings in various stages of demolition. These were the former homes of the residents of Fengdu, most of whom had been evicted and moved across the river to a new town. There, if the Chinese government was to be believed, they had been installed in new accommodation of sybaritic luxury. In reality, many displaced citizens had received very little in return for their forced relocation, and corrupt local officials had pocketed the compensation of many more. A number of Fengdu residents, especially the elderly, had wound up homeless and still lived among the buildings, squatting in concrete shells while the water washed away the banks. Here and there, thin trails of smoke from the fires of their camps rose into the air, mixing with those of the demolition teams that would soon man the wrecking balls and bulldozers currently lying idle in the mud.

A sweaty climb through the fog brought us to the ticket counter at the top of the embankment. By the gate the tour guides stood screaming instructions into megaphones as a panicked stream of sightseers forced their way inside. 'You pay,' said my tour guide, still waving her flag in the direction of the entrance. 'Thirty yuan.'

'I was told entry was included in my fare.'

'No,' she snapped.

Grudgingly, and with a loud curse on the ancestors of Ronald McDonald, I fished the money from my pocket and entered the compound.

Also known as the 'city of ghosts', the temple complex of Fengdu is modelled on the Chinese vision of hell. As such, it was to prove one of the few attractions I saw along the Yangtze that would live up to its promise, though for reasons that were merely coincidental.

Built on either side of a small mountain valley, Fengdu is a string of gaudy temples connected by stepped paths and a series of bridges and gateways, each offering the visitor a supernatural power, including longevity or fertility but not, tragically, the power to get you out of Fengdu. Straddling the two halves of the mountain is the centrepiece of the complex: an enormous sculpture of an ancient Chinese scholar, referred to in tourist literature I had found in my cabin as the King of Heel.

An obviously recent addition to the landscape, the King of Heel was almost as big as the mountain itself, his head a ten-storey concrete block rising from a high ridge, like an apartment building wearing a hat. His arms were covered walkways running down the hillside, terminating under his chin in a pair of clasped hands as tall as a church spire.

Sculpted steps snaking down the mountain suggested his billowing robes.

As ugly and incongruous as the King of Heel might have seemed, he was entirely in keeping with the character of Fengdu; although almost two thousand years old, most of the complex had been demolished during the Cultural Revolution then rebuilt in the 1980s. For this reason, among others, Fengdu lacked any of the atmosphere normally associated with historical sites. The temples had all the character of mini-golf props; the colours, bright and gaudy, suggested something lead-based and foetus-deforming: the blue a block of toilet freshener, the reds and yellows the inside of a McDonald's cheeseburger. Many of the ceremonial gates were poured concrete. Even the few surviving medieval buildings had been 'restored' to such an extent that almost all traces of antiquity had been scrubbed away,. making them indistinguishable from the modern reproductions. I had been to all-you-can-eat Chinese buffets with more atmosphere than Fengdu. Nevertheless, compelled by some misguided duty to culture, I plodded on, making my way deeper into the complex.

At the top of the stone stairs by the entrance gate, I paused to take in the view of the river. Another fifteen or so boats had arrived, tethered in groups of three to pontoon jetties.

Led by a division of megaphone-wielding guides, thousands of tourists walked the damp paths and climbed the steps. Through the fog, the stream of baseball-capped humanity trudging through the ruins of the demolished city was a haunting, apocalyptic tableau: the day after Hiroshima or the exodus from some future Egypt. It was a romantic idyll, quickly destroyed by the crushing realities of the approaching crowds and the pervasive din of megaphones.

The full horrors of Chinese tourism are not easily conveyed—imagine a prisoner-of-war camp with the inmates in matching baseball caps, or a cruel futuristic reality show in which contestants must engage in deadly combat to win snow-domes and T-shirts that read *My dad went to Fengdu and all he got me was this lousy T-shirt.*

As someone who believes the purpose of travel is to invert normal laws of daily routine by getting as far away from other people as possible, the Chinese tendency to group en masse is baffling. Initially I had reasoned that, with so many people, they just couldn't help running into one another. After a few months, however, I was convinced that the Chinese congregate in massive crowds not because they can't avoid it, but because they like it. Wave a flag in China and you'll soon be guaranteed to have three thousand people trailing you. Add a megaphone and you could get them to do anything. There were occasions when if you'd told me that the Long March or the invasion of Tibet were just sightseeing tours gone wrong, I'd have believed you.

In China, the cruel Darwinian imperatives of the mob overwhelm all other considerations. Personal space, the freedom to move at one's own leisure, respiratory function: these were all very far down the list for the average Chinese tourist. The single-mindedness of the crowd was awe-inspiring. No one strayed; stragglers were harshly dealt with; obedience to their megaphone-wielding overlords was absolute. Seeing these shoving seas of baseball caps the mind moved inevitably to anthropomorphic metaphors: swarms of locusts, herds of cattle, a frantic school of fish dodging a shark. As the tour groups raced up the stairs and began to overtake, I imagined myself as a mortally wounded animal, lying immobile on the jungle floor, watching with terror the approach of ravenous swarms of soldier ants.

Within the gates of the Fengdu complex, the structures became a series of increasingly compact courtyards, each connected by stepped paths and gardens lined with sculptures of various after-life characters. Most alarming of these was a series of muscular concrete demons in a wide spectrum of garish colours. Some were grotesque caricatures of animal spirits; an ox, horse or fish. Others were simply deformed, their oversized mouths revealing rows of broken teeth, their heads lumpy with horns and growths. Each brandished a different weapon, like sci-fi gladiators.

With the crowds gaining, I ran up the steps towards the top of the mountain. At the higher altitudes the mist grew thicker as the chorus of megaphones dimmed behind me. The gardens here were prettier, the trees fuller, the statuary less lurid. Little warning signs dotted the flowerbeds, their messages ranging from the reproachful—*Please pay more attention to the grass flowers and lives*—to cryptic aphorisms of almost Confucian obscurity: *Ecological protection ties everybody's heart*, and *Caring the flowers and trees purifying our hearts and souls*.

Contemplating the prettiness of the gardens and the rising tides of muddy water below, it was difficult not to be struck by the ironies of Chinese ecology: here was a society that saw no contradiction in destroying one of the world's most beautiful ecosystems only to compensate by warning people not to touch the topiary. In the relative peace of the garden, however, political objections soon faded. The buildings in these higher reaches were no more beautiful than elsewhere in Fengdu but had the grace, at least, of being empty. For a moment, illusory as I knew it to be, I felt I had found in this misty landscape some hint of the China of my imagination, the celestial, harmonious kingdom unsullied by aluminium factories, concrete temples and the constant competitive cries of the megaphone.

'Fuck you, you fuckin' cunt!'

The voice was muffled at first, but grew in clarity as the Irish brothers emerged through the portal of a nearby temple.

'*You* fuck yourself, cunt.'

Liam strode ahead while his brother scowled in the background, his fists clenched by his side, his wild stringy hair falling about his face.

'Alright?' said Liam.

'This place fuckin' sucks,' roared Fintan, kicking up a stony wave of gravel. 'Feng-doo, fuck you!' he cried, running off in the direction of a distant courtyard, his army greatcoat trailing behind him with a superhero flutter. Liam said nothing, just sat down on the wall beside me and ground his toe into the gravel, as if killing something very small.

Moments later, the first megaphones began to echo up the stairs. Within a couple of minutes the courtyard was a rolling sea of humanity, the frantic twitching of red flags all that could be seen above the wall of spray jackets and baseball caps.

During my time in China I was to form a few early prejudices which, despite being wide-ranging generalisations of a moderately unkind nature that skirted dangerously close to bigotry, would prove, almost without exception, to be true—among them the fact that the Chinese are, without doubt, the worst-dressed people in the world. Characterised by a bold disregard for any formal aesthetic laws, Chinese fashion is a rich pageant of high-voltage colour and contrasting texture, all informed by an attitude towards manmade fibres that can only be described as permissive. Human technology had yet to invent the vinyl too shiny, the lycra too sheer, the knitwear too flammable to prove unwearable by the Chinese middle class.

As I travelled across the country, I was continually astounded by the radical sartorial liberties of China's bourgeoisie. Once, on a street in Shanghai, I saw two women, possibly twins, wearing crushed velvet tracksuits—one in crimson, the other midnight blue—teamed with matching yellow pumps and gold parkas emblazoned with the Versace Medusa logo and the word *Loverly* arching across the shoulders, the look complemented by lacquered perms piled high into shaggy nests and a pair of parasols printed with poorly drawn Disney cartoons. Spotted in say, New York, their outfits might have marked them as members of some radical new punk movement. In China they were a pair of housewives, off for a spot of shopping before picking up the kids from soccer practice.

Tourism gave the Chinese special licence to indulge their passion for all things clashing and synthetic. White patent-leather shoes were teamed with velvet leggings in maroon and bottle-green. Men in Adidas track pants shuffled along in scuffed burgundy loafers, gold tassels flopping from side to side. Pink spray jackets and grey slacks recalled the opening ceremony of some forgotten Olympics.

The must-have item for women this season—well represented aboard the *Lady Water*—was a synthetic mohair-look sweater cinched about the elbow and waist with thin bands of black vinyl, giving the strange jointed look of a caterpillar. One matron, straining for a view of a distant temple, teamed a maroon velvet blouse with a yellow windbreaker, stiletto knee boots and a pair of voluminous jodhpurs, the entire ensemble complemented by ropes of gold jewellery and lucky charms. At any point she might have been off to sail a catamaran, ride a steeplechase or turn tricks by the docks.

The ubiquitous baseball cap offered more opportunities for self-expression, the various styles and materials distinguishing subtle striations of class. Passengers from the most expensive ships wore fitted caps of silky material, some embroidered with the names of their vessels in extravagant calligraphy: serious-looking businessmen wandered about, their foreheads emblazoned with the words *Princess* or *Victoria Queen*. Their wives wore matching spray jackets with embroidery across the shoulders, giving them the look of 1950s teenyboppers. Poorer passengers were distinguished by caps in flimsy material with adjustable bands, each group identified by a different colour. Some had brims that contrasted with the crowns. Others wore caps divided into segments of red and yellow, echoing the fashion for harlequin pants among their tour leaders.

For a time, I watched the endless stream of tour groups climb the stairs and feed into the temples. Like oil paints on a pool of water, slicks of orange, yellow and fluorescent green met, mingled and coalesced. It didn't take long for the atmosphere to become claustrophobic. Bidding farewell to Liam I made my way back down the mountain, pausing only to turn and watch his brother mount a high wall and kick stones into the crowds, screaming into the foggy abyss.

'Feng-doo, fuck you! Feng-doo, fuck you!'

The day continued at a gruelling pace. After lunch there was another excursion, this time to inspect the Shibaozhai temple, a medieval wooden pavilion clinging to a sheer cliff further downstream. With great reluctance, but nursing the naive hope that this attraction would prove more rewarding than the last, I allowed myself to be bundled along with the crowds. I needn't have bothered. In almost every respect the trip differed little from that to Fengdu: the same crowds climbed the same steps listening to commentary at the same pitch before purchasing the same baseball hats and silken pyjamas from gift shops by the exit.

In some ways Shibaozhai was even more depressing than Fengdu. The rising water was more palpable here and the poverty of the surrounding countryside more desperate. From the top of the temple I could see the vegetable gardens of the local people being turned to mud; their livelihoods ruined, they had no other choice but to scrounge a living from tourists. As we disembarked, dozens of wild-looking men, and several equally fevered women, rushed through the knee-deep swamp to offer palanquin rides to the summit. When I refused they bowed and tugged at my sleeves, as if they were lepers and I a saint with miraculous healing powers.

Although considered one of China's great architectural wonders, Shibaozhai could not be saved from the waters.

Its conservation had inspired several ambitious, albeit utterly depressing, plans including the possibility of ringing the building in a huge concrete weir. When I suggested to the tour guide that this might detract from the temple she laughed as if I had said something very stupid and said, 'No! It will be more beautiful. Shibaozhai will be island. *Beautiful* island.' She gestured towards the muddy, swollen river. 'All the Yangtze is more beautiful now.'

Evening brought the return of Mr Snack to the cabin. A small bow and a quick removal of his shoes was a prelude to his evening ritual of plastic packets and television. It was not the first time I had seen him that day. After the excursion to Shibaozhai I had sat on the roof deck and watched him among the other members of his tour group; some of the older people practised tai-chi while the rest sat in groups, talking, smoking and taking turns to spit off the side. Mr Snack did not appear to join any of the conversations, preferring to sit alone, stiff-backed, in a plastic chair, staring off the bow.

This seeming preference for solitude was intriguing. Was Mr Snack merely shy, I wondered, or was there some deeper mystery? How to explain, for instance, his apparent single status? An unmarried man in China of his generation was unusual, so where was Mrs Snack: at home? Dead? Could it be that Mr Snack's journey aboard the *Lady Water* might have had some purpose other than mere sightseeing?

I began to speculate wildly: Mr Snack was a Communist Party spy; on the run for murder; an undercover quality-control officer from *Lady Water* head office. As I watched him sitting cross-legged on his bed, chewing his way through a packet of deep-fried squid tentacles, I couldn't help but wonder whether the lack of communication between us was solely the fault of the language barrier.

Consistent with Mr Snack's preference for solitude was the fact he never went to dinner. Of course, on the *Lady Water*, this was extremely sensible. Each night the ritual was the same: the hacking and spitting, the prison wardens manning their cauldrons, the mysterious room full of privileged diners. As I made my way past their tables I lingered enviously, salivating at the sight of their mountains of food. Who were these people? I had no idea. But as I stood and watched them, lost in their world of private pleasure, it seemed they might be ghosts of long-dead passengers, apparitions of happier times aboard the *Lady Water*, appearing only to heighten the suffering of the present.

The Irishmen had returned for dinner. Sitting in the same spot as the previous evening they scowled into their prison trays, their meals supplemented by portions of a melon, chopped up with a bowie knife.

'Have some,' said Fintan stabbing into the fruit with Norman Bates motions.

'Maybe later,' I said.

'Have some fuckin' melon.'

Obediently, I took a mangled slice of pulp from the end of the knife.

Despite the introduction of weaponry, dinner with the brothers was less draining than the previous evening. Fintan's brooding fury had been replaced with a manic talkativeness, aided by enormous bottles of beer. By the time we finished, the dining room was completely empty, the canteen women were mopping the floor and we were close to very drunk.

'Let's go sing karaoke,' said Fintan, sheathing his knife.

That the *Lady Water* had a karaoke lounge at all struck me as strange—like a fully equipped day spa in a maximum-security prison. The scene inside was no less unlikely.

In a hidden stairwell, under a string of blinking lights, a wood-panelled door opened to reveal a room steeped in darkness. At its centre a man sang a Chinese song into a microphone. From a ring of sticky vinyl couches, a small audience watched, their faces splashed in the weak light of an oversized television. A karaoke video featured a woman strolling through a grove of blossoming trees. As the song came to its conclusion the audience leaped to their feet and cheered. Fintan joined in, cheering more wildly than everybody else and waving a large beer bottle over his head. The audience reared back in alarm, but the man with the microphone was in party mode. Grabbing the Irishman around the shoulders he began a new round of song. Together the pair swayed drunkenly while Fintan shouted profanities, drank his beer and kicked in time to the martial beat of the music. At the end of their performance the audience gave another standing ovation while the man with the microphone hugged his new friend and raised their joined fists in triumph.

The singer returned to his companions while Fintan busied himself with the karaoke machine. 'I want some fuckin' Sinatra,' he cried as he twiddled knobs and mashed his fist into buttons, oblivious to the disapproving looks of the crowd. 'Where is the fuckin' Sinatra?'

On a couch next to the main party, Liam and I sipped our beer and made nods of acknowledgement to the others. They gave us forced smiles before returning to their examination of the folder containing the song list.

It was at this point I noticed something unusual: of the seven or so people in their gathering, at least five were women, all considerably younger than the pair of drunken men in their company. In fact, now I thought about it, almost all the passengers aboard the *Lady Water*, other than the Irishmen and myself, were middle-aged or older. The only other younger people were the tour guides who, outside of their guiding duties or yelling at me in my bedroom at 3 a.m., I hadn't seen anywhere else: not in the dining room, on the deck or even in the corridors. To see them here, therefore, struck me as odd—in part that the karaoke lounge would be their only escape from the confines of their quarters, but mostly because, from my (admittedly limited) observations, single girls in China, unless they were rich westernised types, didn't go to bars and get drunk with older men, sing karaoke and flutter and fuss over them as if they were show dogs. Women in China who did this were known by a great variety of names, most of which, I'm fairly certain, did not translate—even ironically—as 'tour guide'.

Unable to find any music to his taste on the karaoke machine, Fintan settled for a Chinese song. The fact he could not speak Chinese was no hindrance. For the next minute he sang a stream of vaguely 'Chinese'-sounding words into the microphone: '*Nee shah ching wah!*' Oddly, his audience didn't seem offended by this boorish behaviour so much as bemused. I could only suppose they assumed he was singing in English or, perhaps, some other unidentified language. Maybe they were just afraid.

After a little more of Fintan's serenade, the second male companion got up from his seat and wrested the microphone back. To my surprise and relief, the Irishman gave up without a fight. Bowing to confused applause and rousing the crowd with cries of 'Thank you, China!' he staggered off to join his brother and me on the couch.

After a quick adjustment of the karaoke machine, the man began to sing a song in English, 'Close to You' by the Carpenters. It was popular in China: in my time in the country the only two English-language songs I heard on a regular basis were it and 'Bridge over Troubled Water', which I had once heard as the soundtrack to a television advertisement for what had appeared to be a vaginal douche.

For a time I sat listening to the man. He sang well but in a weirdly disconnected way, as if he had learned the sounds but not their meanings. Halfway through, to my surprise, one of the women leaned across and, in fractured English, emboldened by alcohol, said, 'I love this song. Who sings this song?'

I explained it was by Karen Carpenter, but that she had died in the early 1980s.

'The 1980s …' She shook her head in bewilderment. She seemed shocked the song was so old. 'How did she die?'

'She had anorexia.'

Her brow furrowed.

'She wouldn't eat,' I said, spooning phantom food to my mouth.

Her look of bewilderment was absolute. 'She would not eat?'

'Yes. She wouldn't eat and she died of starvation.'

She nodded thoughtfully and for a moment stared at the ground with melancholy bewilderment. Then, leaning in, she said more quietly, 'I suck your cock?'

Nights on the *Lady Water* were damp and silent. After dinner, the corridors emptied and the chilly fog on the decks discouraged lingering. Pockets of life remained, mostly around the foyer, where a few men sat on couches smoking and dropping their butts into the brass pots. For the most part, however, people retreated to their rooms immediately after dinner and stayed there.

My encounter with the girl in the karaoke lounge had unnerved me. Why, I was not entirely sure: it wasn't as if I hadn't had similar offers in other parts of the world, some of which I'd have gladly accepted if not for the threat of imprisonment, venereal disease or the possibility I might arrive home and open my bag to find some stowaway rent boy curled up inside. It was the subterfuge that disturbed me, an underhandedness that seemed to suggest something sinister was afoot aboard the *Lady Water*.

In the dark empty corridors a haunted atmosphere took over the ship. Anchored in the swift current, the boat shifted from side to side, making doors creak and springing open empty life-jacket cupboards at heart-stopping intervals. The damp seemed to be in everything—not just the floors but the walls, railings, even my clothes. Condensation formed on the mirrors and dripped from the sparkling stalactites of the bronze chandelier. It was as if the damp were a living entity, oozing out of the ship's pores, an ectoplasm that had come to claim the living for the grave.

The *Lady Water* was divided into three classes. First-class I was, of course, intimately acquainted with. Second, which was on the deck below, I had seen during a visit to the Irishmen to borrow a bottle-opener. Their accommodation was the same as mine but with a pair of bunk beds in place of the singles and no fancy extras, like phlegm-protecting slippers. Third-class took up most of the middle and all the lower deck and looked like an illegal people-smuggling operation.

The rooms contained four sets of steel-frame bunks separated by a forearm of space, almost every square inch filled with an archaeological stratum of plastic bags, cigarette cartons and clanking bottles of Chinese wine. Outside, on the small area of deck that served as a balcony, yet more bags were piled into stacks while rows of singlets and underpants flapped a nautical distress signal in the breeze.

Everyone in third-class smoked continuously. From each doorway wafted constant, eye-watering columns of smoke that reduced visibility in the hallways to mere inches and turned the cabins themselves into nicotine saunas negotiable only by the power of touch.

Despite their discomforts, there was a pleasant communal cheeriness to these rooms. In the evenings, men in their underwear cracked open bottles of beer while women handed out snacks, fished from bottomless laundry bags. Snatches of laughter mingled with jolly toasts. Rousing songs sung into portable karaoke machines emanated into the corridors until late. Given the lonely, frigid atmosphere of my own cabin, it was easy to find myself jealous, if only momentarily, of these people and their raucous proletarian amusements. Standing by the doors, I nursed fantasies of making friends, of being adopted into their cosy families and fed tidbits from laundry bags. I imagined myself sitting in the centre of a ring of smiling faces, proclaiming toasts with oversized beer bottles and performing party tricks to the delight of all. Fathers would slap my back and break open special bottles of rice wine to honour the occasion. Wizened grandmothers would pinch my cheeks and declare me one of their own. Perhaps there would be an invitation to join them in the village after our journey. There we would sit by a coal fire into the night, singing karaoke, eating home-cooked food and recalling the golden days aboard the *Lady Water*.

In reality, attempts to introduce myself were humiliatingly unsuccessful. Entreating smiles and bows were met only with blank silent faces, caught momentarily in a rictus of alarm, before a rapid retreat into the impenetrable fog of tobacco. One room closed the door on me as I waved hello, as if I were a stalker or child snatcher, a dangerous, apefaced criminal on the prowl. To be fair, given the events in the dining room the previous evening, this might not have been an entirely unfair assumption. Nevertheless, the rejection and hurt were real, and as I wandered aimlessly along the corridors I could only resign myself to solitude.

The lowest class of all on the *Lady Water*—if it qualified as a class—was reserved for the tour guides. I had discovered their accommodation while investigating the front of the ship: opening a door at the end of the middle deck revealed two dozen people nestled among a shantytown of bedding and laundry lines. They slept on the damp floor in rows of three, most without a mattress. Women seemed to outnumber men but they all slept side by side, some propped up in bed talking or eating pot noodles. In one corner someone had strung up a sheet to form a changing room.

As I stood in the doorway, a dozen wary gazes met mine. For a moment I considered introducing myself—perhaps some spoke enough English for a conversation?—but soon decided against it. The general impression was of having stumbled unwittingly into a members-only bar in some not entirely welcoming part of town. As quickly as I had arrived, I retreated from their private world.

Back in my room Mr Snack was eating a packet of dried noodles and watching a soap opera. The fish spirit had made an appearance and now seemed to have kidnapped the pregnant princess. Inside his grotto lair, she was forced to eat grubs and weed while water dripped on her head. I was filled with empathy for her predicament.

As I sat on my bed, Mr Snack offered a little bow of acknowledgement. I returned his greeting, noting a row of black nylon socks he had hung to dry over the side table and bedposts. Seeing me regard them he put down his packet and reached for one on my side of the table. I indicated he should leave it. With a nod of gratitude he retreated to his reclining position and continued chewing, his eyes fixed on the television. Touched as I was by this concession to my comfort, I still nursed a certain antipathy towards Mr Snack: what was supposed to be a recuperative, restful journey was proving a punishing endurance test. Mr Snack, with his spitting, his socks, his snoring and his aloof, vaguely persecuted manner—as if *I* were the one that ought to be regarded as a resentfully tolerated imposition—was just the rancid cherry on an already repellent cake.

Slipping on an eye mask I did my best to detach myself from my environment. To no avail; the *Lady Water* invaded everything: my sheets, my lungs, my mind itself. The sounds of the night were a taunting conspiracy. On the television, the fish spirit was engaged in a violent kung fu battle. Outside, rain beat down into the Yangtze. In his bed, Mr Snack rustled and crunched. As the ship rocked and creaked in the storm, the ghosts of the *Lady Water* knocked mournfully at the door.

Day 3

At 3.30 a.m. there was a familiar thudding. Opening one eye I was confronted, again, by the triumphant smirk of the tour guide. 'You must wake up,' she said, fingering her clipboard. 'You see gorges. Very beautiful. Wake up.' With the slamming of the door, Mr Snack rose, offered a tiny bow and retreated to the bathroom. As the morning's hawking reached its crescendo I sat up, cleared the sleep from my eyes and began massaging my legs back to life. By my window the magnificent soaring marble cliffs of the first and, some say, greatest of the Three Gorges was slipping past. At least this is what I presumed; everything was still in complete darkness, the organisers of this journey not, apparently, regarding as important the timing of the ship's passage with sunrise.

By the time I reached the roof deck the light had improved to a leaden grey but the mist was still impenetrable. Groups of thwarted tourists stood about in the freezing air, pointing into the fog and talking over a pair of tour leaders positioned at opposite ends of the deck, who were screeching into megaphones and gesticulating at nothing. A number of sightseers, not easily put off, stood with video cameras and mobile phones held before their faces, staring intently at grey LED screens.

At breakfast, neither Mandy and Tina nor the Irishmen were anywhere to be seen. I ate alone, supplementing my porridge with bits of chicken from what remained of the carcass I had bought on the dock in Chongqing. As I tore the final shreds from the bony breast its black eyes stared reproachfully.

The day's timetable was long. Soon after breakfast we would pass through the Wu Gorge, the second of the Three Gorges. After that we would disembark and take a tour of a tributary of the river. Deciding to beat the crowds, I made my way upstairs to the roof deck. Outside, it was cool and misty. The banks of the river rolled past, green hills disappearing slowly under the rising muddy waters. Taking a plastic chair, I commandeered a position by the prow and for a moment watched the scenery in glorious isolation.

A squall of feedback marked the arrival of the first crush of passengers. In less than two minutes the entire deck was covered with what seemed to be hundreds of people, all wearing coloured baseball caps. Around the periphery, tour leaders shouted into megaphones and pointed at rocks rising from the banks. No one looked directly at anything, staring instead into the miniature windows of their LED screens with all the intensity of detectives peering through magnifying glasses.

Back in my room, Mr Snack was gone. Across the hall a familiar techno soundtrack of zips and clicks was audible through the half-opened door of Mandy and Tina's room. I knocked gingerly.

'Who is it?' The voice sounded accusing and alarmed.

'It's just me.'

The door creaked open. Tina's head appeared around the edge. 'Oh,' she said. For a moment we stared at each other in silence, like two lone soldiers who have crossed paths in no-man's-land and must now decide whether to shoot or cautiously agree to go their separate ways.

'I'm sorry,' I said. 'I was just wondering whether you would be going to lunch. I didn't see you at breakfast.'

'Hm,' said Tina, as if this were a pretty unlikely pretext for a social call. For a moment I imagined myself as Mandy and Tina might see me: a young male stranger aboard a cruise ship, travel-soiled, bearded and not wholly reputable-looking. No one could blame them for being suspicious, and not just because I looked like a rapist on a wanted poster. Why was I so keen to befriend Mandy and Tina? Because they were the only people aboard the *Lady Water* I could talk to who didn't own a bowie knife, or because in them I sensed something intriguing my curiosity would not let rest?

'No. Thank you for your invitation, Brendan,' said Tina, closing her eyes in a condescending expression of finality, as if I were some barefoot farm boy making a fool of myself with the plantation owner's daughter. 'We're not going anywhere near that dining room again.' She shook her head emphatically. 'No way. Forget it.' She made a sweeping gesture with her arms.

'Okay,' I said, and there was another silence.

Just as I was about to say my goodbyes there was a sudden rustling from within the room followed by a sharp shriek. 'Tina! Tina!' came the cry from behind the door. 'Tina, come help!' Tina turned and dashed inside. Compelled by the list of the boat, the door began to draw shut. Emboldened by a sense that my services might be required, coupled with the opportunity to further insinuate myself into the narrative of their lives, I jammed my foot in the door, pushed it open and went inside.

Mandy was sitting on a bed, looking distressed. Over her, Tina was standing, hunched, holding a large make-up bag, the teeth of its thick stainless steel zip biting a decent-sized clump of her friend's hair.

'Oh, Tina! Be careful. Tina, it hurts,' wailed Mandy as her friend pulled at the zip.

'Just hold still,' scolded Tina. 'I think I can unzip it without ripping out too much.'

Mandy gave a few more cries of 'Tina!' before bringing her hands across her eyes in a gesture of despairing self-reproach.

'Can I help?' I asked.

Tina ignored me. 'How did you *do* this?' she demanded.

Mandy launched into a panicked explanation punctuated by yelps of pain as Tina yanked at the zipper. 'I think we're going to have to cut it out,' announced Tina with a schoolmistressy tone that came close to spiteful satisfaction. At this Mandy gave a hooting, scornful laugh and flung her hands in the air.

'Here, hold this,' Tina said to me. I took the bag while she ran about the room, madly releasing deadbolts and unzipping bags. 'Where are the scissors?' she cried from the bathroom, rummaging through a clacking assortment of toiletries.

'Tina, they're not there,' cried Mandy. Tina remerged and began to rifle through a dozen pockets secured by steel cable. 'Tina, I'm trying to tell you,' said Mandy, staring at her friend through a web of tangled hair. 'They're in the gosh-darn bag!' To emphasise the point she tapped the bag I held in my hand.

'Oh, Mandy,' cried Tina with the kind of exasperated affection of a parent scolding a child with its head stuck in a bucket. Taking the bag from me she gave a last desperate yank at the zip. Mandy issued a high screech of pain.

'Wait,' I said suddenly. 'I've got some in my room.' I ran across the corridor and returned with my scissors. Wordlessly, Tina took them and began to snip at the trapped hair. As Mandy held the make-up bag with both hands, like an offering, feathery showers of hair fell to her lap.

In a few seconds the procedure was complete. The bag was sitting on the bed, a voodoo tuft of Mandy's blonde-grey hair poking out from between its evil teeth. There was a pause; Tina stood, scissors in hand. Mandy carefully collected the hair from her lap then got to her feet. 'Oh, Tina,' she said, bursting into tears. 'It's all been so terrible.'

'There, there,' said Tina as she embraced Mandy, the latter still clutching her strands of hair. 'It will be alright. You're getting flustered again.'

With Tina still rubbing her friend's back I quietly slipped out the door, leaving the pair to their private consolations.

⁓

As we docked, the previous day's scene was repeated. The passengers of the *Lady Water* surged across the gangplank and onto a temporary wooden jetty, slick with mud. Towering above, a huge concrete embankment loomed, protecting the new city from the river. Following the crowds, I made my way along the muddy path towards a shantytown of gift shops huddled around a flotilla of ferryboats. Docked at regular intervals along the shore were a number of other cruise ships. Some were not unlike the

Lady Water, although none seemed quite so bedraggled. Others were enormous luxury liners with glass-encased viewing platforms and swimming pools, at least one of which I felt sure I had seen in Ronald McDonald's brochure. A couple were historically themed, crowned with ornate Chinese roofs. One had been modelled into a golden dragon, a mouth at its prow containing the control deck. From inside the open jaws little men in white crew uniforms surveyed the dock, like the ghosts of past meals.

Feeling envious, I made my way past these floating palaces and tramped through the gift stalls towards the dock. As the passengers of the luxury ships walked down the gangplanks of the ferries, their excursion over, those from the *Lady Water* forced their way up. Heedless of safety, they barged around the stragglers and claimed the few seats in a ruthless game of musical chairs that left me standing, unsheltered, on the upper deck.

As we moved away the rain began to fall. By the time we had begun to wend our way downriver it was heavy enough to send rivulets down my coat. After travelling a while past steep embankments dotted with drowning farms, we arrived at our first stop, an island created by the rising waters.

Up a flight of stairs we came upon a field lined with gift stalls selling the usual array of souvenirs: cheap silk products, old photographs, fans, Mao memorabilia, chipped pottery and wooden children's dolls with jointed limbs, prominent genitals and serrated teeth set in demonic grins. Behind these stalls, under a covered walkway, stood an exhibition of sorts—dozens of enormous crystals, each prized for its unusual shape and properties of good fortune. Some stood on rickety wooden tables accompanied by dusty labels in Chinese. Others were locked behind glass in what appeared to be old medicine cabinets. For a moment I joined the others in a dutiful inspection of the collection, noting with particular interest the quartz sculpture cleverly fashioned into a rearing stallion, an erection half the size of its amber-coloured body sprouting from its belly.

Exiting the exhibition, I strolled for a while about the muddy flats, unsure of the purpose of our visit to this place. From a distance the stallholders beckoned, eyeing me hungrily. Suddenly, a charging platoon emerged from the mist and rain. The interlopers were a bedraggled collection of men and women, the mud on their clothes, bandaged hands and shoeless feet marking them as farmers from the distant fields. Surrounding us, they held out boxes of pottery wrapped in newspapers. With great force they pressed their bundles on us. Seeing this, the stallholders began to scream in protest, signalling that they should return to the fields. For a moment the farmers hesitated, obviously afraid: who knew which local don controlled these concessions? Desperation, however, made them bold. After a spirited shouting match, the stallholders accepted defeat.

The poverty of the farmers was shocking, the worst I had seen in China. Their skin was dry and taut, their jawlines prominent. Some of the women seemed to be losing hair in clumps. Plastered on their faces were fixed grins so beseeching they verged on crazed, as if I might have spat in their faces or kicked their shins and they'd just keep smiling and forcing little bowls into my hands. The entire scene was wretched and depressing and, not for the first time on my travels, I found myself in the uncomfortable position of having all the power.

A man dumped a box at my feet. From it he forced upon me piles of bowls wrapped in filthy newspaper. Resigned to my fate, I kneeled down and began to sift through his collection. It was the usual assortment, but when I plucked a delicate blue bowl from the bottom and took a closer look a near riot ensued. Dozens of hands proffered crockery, pawed at my jacket and dropped objects into my lap. It distressed me too much to buy only one thing from such obviously desperate people. In a guilty panic, I began to hand out notes for what soon tallied a half-dozen pieces.

Fending off clawing hands, I eventually made my retreat. Down at the dock I bought some little fried fish on skewers. Even as I handed the man my few cents a woman tugged at my sleeve and waved bits of crockery by my face, smiling and nodding as I tried to ignore her.

Escaping to the ferry, I dumped my purchases and began to tear at the fish. It tasted like burnt hair. This was famine food, consumed for protein alone. I managed two and offered the remains to an old man beside me. He waved his hand in refusal and gave a little giggle, whether out of embarrassment or disgust I could not tell. When no one was looking I threw the remains overboard and watched the bamboo sticks spin as eels broke the surface to snap at them with their horrid black snouts.

The boat pushed on. Slowly we passed bright green fields combed with crops; abandoned-looking sheds stood watch over gardens being swallowed by the rising water. Soon the farms gave way and the boat entered a spectacular canyon, the first time this journey had made good on its promise of natural beauty.

This new stretch prompted an orgy of videoing. The passengers wandered about the deck, staring blank-faced at the scenery through the screens of their cameras, pausing only to spit off the boat. One cretinous, slack-jawed teenaged girl wearing a sweater detailed with Donald Duck patches physically pushed me from my position by the railings to better film the scenery. While she filmed, her adoring parents, each armed with their own cameras, filmed her. As I watched the scene a man stood not two feet away and videoed me from head to toe as if conducting a futuristic medical scan.

After floating between the mountains for half an hour, we arrived at a dock surrounded by dozens of long wooden motorboats. As we alighted the rain began in earnest. Shrieking, people ran onto the boats and sheltered under the blue plastic coverings. Slow to realise what was happening, I was forced to settle for a seat at the outer edge of the boat where the plastic stopped and water cascaded down in a sheet on my head. As we took off, I saw Mandy and Tina sitting in another boat cloaked in matching plastic ponchos, looking like grim yellow monks.

The tour through the gorge was scenic but difficult to enjoy. My attempts to direct the rain off my head by holding the edge of the plastic were making my arm numb and the woman beside me was making pointed protests with her elbow. I gestured to the roof by way of explanation but she just turned, said something loudly to her companion, and held her video camera in front of my face.

As we moved deeper into the canyon the scenery grew yet more beautiful. In these deep channels life was abundant. Monkeys—the first wild animals I had seen in China—ran up and down the cliffs. Birds squawked on high branches. Ferns dripped thin trails of silver water. The vegetation sprouting from the walls and peaks of the canyons threw into high relief the barrenness of the Yangtze banks. Only now did I realise how denuded the land was, as if it had been used and used until it had nothing left to give.

For a moment, the rain eased and I could sit comfortably. As we pulled away from the other boats, the engines and megaphones dulled. It became quieter, serene almost. An old man appeared, walking along a treacherous path by the banks of the river. Bent-backed and with a long grey beard, he carried a barrel-sized bundle of sticks over his shoulders.

The monkeys, the old man and the forest: it seemed a scene straight from an ink scroll, and for a moment I allowed myself to think that I had found some hint of the China I had dreamed of in those technicolour reveries.

Suddenly, in a gesture that brought murmurs from the onlookers, the old man dropped his bundle. Lifting his head and turning towards the boat he broke into a booming folk song. The crowd roared with laughter at the deception. Beside me, the woman with the camera brought it back in front of my face. Once he had finished, the old man bowed to acknowledge the thunderous applause from the boats.

Narrating the next scene, the tour guides yelled into megaphones as a pair of country maidens in silken costumes joined the singer. In the cat-like register of Chinese opera, the three began a new song with all the mechanical enthusiasm of condemned prisoners forced to entertain a fickle emperor. Halfway through the recital, the rain returned. As I tried to draw the canopy over me, my neighbour elbowed me, hard.

By the time we returned to the ferry I was soaked to the skin. The journey back through the canyon was scenic but taxing. While admiring the view, I was accosted by a girl who stood beside me while her companions took a photograph. Seeing this, others began to queue for the privilege. By the end of the ordeal I had posed with at least half a dozen. Normally I wouldn't have minded—I am a large and obvious target for the curiosity of people in many countries, especially Asia, and have gladly submitted myself to similar requests on numerous occasions. The pushy manners of my interlopers, however, were trying my patience. One after the other they lined up to cling to my arms, some demanding second and third pictures after the initial was deemed unsatisfactory. None made any token of requesting my consent. Few, indeed, even appeared to acknowledge my existence as a sentient being, regarding me more as if I were a rock formation or a man in a costume at a theme park. As I stood gritting my teeth—a middle-aged woman in a purple mohair sweater with gold epaulets gripping my arm—all I could do was comfort myself with the thought that this would be my last day aboard the *Lady Water*.

Keen to avoid further attention from my public, I made my way down to the front of the boat. Here, past the driver's cabin, guarded by a sign reading DRIVE ZONE, DON'T BOTHER, I found a small area, blissfully empty except for two others engaged in cheerful conversation. For a moment, I didn't recognise them: the only hint of familiarity, a blue vinyl jacket.

Leaning against the railings in a relaxed posture, Mr Snack was deep in a lively conversation with the tour guide—the same who had asked me to leave the room and now took spiteful delight in waking me every morning. In her harlequin pants, clipboard hugged to her chest and a megaphone slung over one shoulder, she listened with what seemed genuine appreciation. As Mr Snack raised his hands in comic frustration and signalled into the distance the tour guide smiled and even laughed. For a moment I watched, but as soon as we made eye contact their cheerfulness ended. Mr Snack grew introverted and hushed. I smiled and nodded; he returned my greeting with a single, defeated-looking nod. Turning to me, the tour guide gave a tight smile, screwing her eyes shut as if she had been pinched someplace sensitive.

My sense of intruding was palpable, but I felt no need to offer them privacy. Indeed, considering the number of times they had invaded my life, I regarded it as a small form of revenge.

'How are you?' I asked the guide brightly.

Her eyes narrowed and she said something to Mr Snack. He looked blankly off into the distance and fiddled with the zip on his blue jacket.

'The gorge is very beautiful,' I said.

'Yes,' she said. 'Tonight you see traditional Chinese history show.' She paused. 'You must buy ticket.'

'I'm sure.'

'Goodbye,' she said and, with that, the pair disappeared back past the driver's cabin and melted into the crowds.

Of course, I could have just been imagining things. The tour guide and Mr Snack were, no doubt, simply friends—I had, on occasion, compared life aboard the *Lady Water* to a hostage situation, and who was to say these two hadn't experienced in one another's company the same kind of deranged Stockholm Syndrome that had brought me together with Mandy and Tina. Yet, as I pondered certain incidents over the last few days, more likely explanations began to assert themselves: the insistence that I should leave my bed, her subsequent antagonism, the scene in the karaoke room, the absence of any Mrs Snack and now the secretive meeting aboard the ferry—all seemed to point to something entirely less innocent.

Was the *Lady Water* a front, I wondered, a hive of opportunistic prostitution, or was Mr Snack having an affair, a prearranged rendezvous ruined by a western interloper? Only one thing was certain: behind his protective wall of soy crisps and pot noodles, Mr Snack nursed a secret and, despite our proximity, I was still no closer to unearthing it.

Back aboard the *Lady Water* lunch was served. Soon we would arrive at the last of the Three Gorges, a sight I anticipated eagerly—partly because it offered the prospect of a leisurely afternoon free of organised activities but mostly because it meant we were only one gorge away from getting off the *Lady Water*. Today, the Irishmen had resurfaced for the midday meal, but they were no more cheerful or less combative.

'I want some fucking meat,' grumbled Fintan.

'Tell us again,' said Liam. 'I didn't hear you the first hundred fuckin' times.'

Anxious to avoid any repeat of earlier scenes, I finished my meal quickly and returned to my room. The cabin was empty, Mr Snack's presence marked only by a small mountain of noodle pots, plastic wrappers and phlegm wads in the wastepaper bin. For a few minutes I read a book in glorious isolation, almost allowing myself to fall into a daydream far removed from a world of drying socks, rice porridge and mucus.

A thump on my door brought me back to the harsh realities of life aboard the *Lady Water*. The tour guide let herself in. 'Tonight Chinese history show,' she announced gesturing with a wad of pink tickets in her hand. 'Forty yuan.'

'I don't want to go,' I said.

She pretended not to understand. Tearing the ticket she pushed it towards me and repeated, 'Forty yuan.' Sighing, I gave her the money. 'Bus tonight,' she said. 'Free tour of dam.'

'Well, that's something,' I said, expressing my astonishment that something on this 'all-inclusive' tour had actually been included.

'No English tour,' she said. 'Chinese only.' And, for a moment, I thought I saw her smile.

The tour guide's visit destroyed my serenity. With her exit, I became suddenly restless and claustrophobic. Taking my book, I made my way to the observation deck. To my surprise, not only had the weather improved—the grey sky now revealing occasional flashes of blue—but the deck was entirely empty. The last of the three gorges, the longest, though least spectacular, was passing by and no one seemed to be interested but me.

For another glorious moment I sat in total isolation, the green cones of the mountaintops lost in whirling currents of mist. Through the smoky atmosphere a thin pagoda appeared on a distant peak, a delicate exclamation point against the grey sky. From this distance it looked very ancient and I found myself hoping that at least this remote structure had escaped the mindless destruction of China's recent past. I wondered how long it would be before someone strung a cable car off it, built a cocktail lounge on top or whether, right now, concrete statues stood guard inside, frightening teams of baseball-capped tourists.

For a few precious minutes, peace reigned, the silence disturbed only by the throb of engines, the rush of water on the hull and the distant toot of boat horns. Just as I found myself able to relax once again, two couples joined me on the deck. I nodded as they took up their positions by the railing. They didn't speak, just stared at the scenery. For a moment I entertained the possibility that these people shared my yearning for solitude and quiet contemplation— fellow seekers of tranquillity, refugees from enforced marches, videography and the constant hectoring of the megaphone. It was not, of course, to be.

With the arrival of the first guide, the foursome, with Pavlovian compliance, took up position in a row of plastic chairs immediately behind me. The guide, standing not three metres away, brought the megaphone to her lips and began to gesture with her flag at various notable rock formations—this one like a horse, that one an ox, the other a profile of some forgotten emperor.

It is difficult to remember but, as I listened to her scream into the megaphone and watched the gymnastic gestures of her flag and the blank looks on the faces of the passengers, I may have started crying.

It was almost dark by the time we docked. On shore, a fleet of buses revved their engines in anticipation. After a short journey we arrived at the edge of the dam. Considering the trying nature of our previous sightseeing, I had no great hopes for this latest expedition, a fact that, in some ways, only heightened the surprise of what awaited us.

Out of the bus we filed in panicked cordons, following the twitching flags of the tour guide. From the lookout I stared. As far as the eye could see, the concrete towers of the half-finished dam marched into the distance. Floodlit yellow in the night, they recalled ancient battlements, the ruins of extinct Titans. Running the length of the dam, thousands of cranes bent and lifted their loads like thin birds picking over a garbage dump. From the building site, mist and dust rose into the air, creating clouds of gold smoke. Insects swarmed around the lamps while birds, their wings in silhouette against the floodlights, swooped to catch them.

Deaf to the tour guides, I wandered closer to the edge. Down below, through one small opening, all the power of the Yangtze seemed to be pouring through. In the dark the water swirled and eddied, muscular and alive, like the surface of some black sun.

In my time aboard the *Lady Water* I had witnessed a number of the disastrous consequences of this project: people evicted from their homes, farmland destroyed, the destruction of one of the world's natural wonders. The Yangtze, ancient and indomitable, had been tamed, like a sad lion in a zoo. I should have been appalled, but I wasn't. Indeed, an entirely unexpected sensation stirred in me now—something close to exhilaration. It was, I realise, absurd to come all this way, to travel the great river, only to be awed by the agent of its destruction. Yet who could help but feel invigorated by the sheer nature-defying, God-challenging hubris required to build something this vast? For a moment I thought of all those desperate farmers I had seen with their broken bowls and bandaged hands and offered a silent apology.

The buses shuttled us to a visitors centre. There we were herded into a gift shop where we could purchase commemorative polo shirts and baseball caps emblazoned with a little image of the dam. Outside, in the flower gardens, Fintan stood on a pile of decorative rocks and addressed the crowd.

'I'm a pugilist and a fighter,' he boomed, punching the air before him. 'Better watch out, motherfuckers, 'cause I'm coming to get ya!'

With that he spread his greatcoat behind him and, gripping it at both corners as if flying, launched himself into the startled crowd. Women squealed with delight and fear as he scattered their tight-knit groups, rival baseball caps crashing and melding. Beside me, Liam watched his brother's manic display, smirking with amusement.

A visit to a Buddhist temple followed; a plaque by the door explained it had been moved to save it from the water. Inside, the atmosphere was relatively calm and serene, the carved pillars and window shades cast expressive shadows across the floor. In the inner sanctum, a handful of monks handed out incense sticks. As I tried to enter, one herded me back out the door with a flutter of his hands. Shocked and dejected as I was by this eviction—the first and only such experience I have had at a Buddhist temple—I could only guess the monks feared attracting attention to their religious activities. Next door, in a concession to the authorities, a bored-looking novice manned a brightly lit shop selling Communist propaganda. As I inspected portraits of Chairman Mao and copies of *The Little Red Book*, he sipped dejectedly on a Coke and stared at the ceiling.

Tomorrow my time aboard the *Lady Water* would end. For that I was grateful; it had been the worst travelling experience of my life, and not merely because of the uncomfortable accommodation, bad food and worse company. This country depressed me. Inhumane, bleak, polluted, nationalistic, money-hungry: you could say that about a lot of places but only China seemed to be proud of it.

China was so full of boasts—biggest, longest, oldest, first—but what was the point when the culmination of your civilisation was a continent-sized industrial park interspersed with huddles of skyscrapers? The past was dead. I didn't mourn it, but was it really necessary to piss on its grave?

Outside the temple, there was a sudden disturbance. Fintan appeared out of the dark, a giant bat with a mane of shaggy blond hair flying through the crowds. 'I'm a pugilist, motherfuckers! A pugilist and a fighter! Outta me way!'

On the television in our room the soap opera continued. The fish spirit had been vanquished and the pregnant princess returned safely to court. All seemed well, but was there a suggestion she was harbouring a secret? As her husband embraced her in celebration of the imminent arrival of what he thought to be their child, the camera zoomed in over his shoulder to capture her hidden expression. Her look of concern was unmistakable: it's one thing when a kid is born with an unexpected hair or eye colour; it's quite another when he has webbed hands, a taste for worms and the power to breathe underwater.

Mr Snack began to pack. One after another the bright stacks of pot noodles and the crinkling packets of soy chips and rice crackers, were loaded into striped laundry bags. The clothes hanging about the room were folded into duffle bags and wheelie cases. Once finished, the luggage stood in a teetering wall by the base of his bed, stacked as high and precise as Incan battlements. Panting in his socks, Mr Snack returned to his reclining position and settled down with a packet of crispy pork intestines and a documentary about coal processing in the north-eastern provinces.

Out in the corridor, a series of sharp words punctuated the muffled bickering of Mandy and Tina. I poked my head out the door to see the pair lugging an enormous case covered in locks and chains. It looked like something the mafia drop off bridges at midnight.

'Take it by the handle,' said Tina to Mandy. 'No the other one … the other one!'

'I'm doing my gosh-darn—pardon my language—my gosh-darn best, Tina!'

'Do you need a hand?' I said.

'They specifically said we could leave it behind the desk,' announced Mandy, her face red, her breaths short. 'That it would be secure! Then, when we get there, Madam Mao over there points to a corner of the foyer and tells us to dump it there—just like that. "I don't think so," I said. "Not with all those shifty-looking guys sitting round, smoking cigarettes and eyeing off anything that's not nailed down. No siree Bob," I said. Think she cared? Think she made an effort for us? Not on your life—we're just the customers, that's all.'

If only to stop her ranting, I took the bag and, with extraordinary physical effort, lifted it into their room. 'What have you got in here?' I asked, swinging the case onto the floor with a thump. 'A body?'

Either uncomprehending of or unamused by my admittedly well-worn joke, the pair shot one another a nervous glance before busying themselves again with their luggage.

'If you'd like,' I said, 'I can help you in the morning with the case. It will be tough to get that thing off the ship.'

'Well thank you, Brendan,' said Mandy. 'Now here's a nice young man.' She turned to Tina and gestured dramatically. 'Helpful!' While her friend spoke, Tina regarded me with her customary look of faint suspicion. She, I had come to believe, was the business end of this partnership.

'So where are you off to next?' I asked.

'Back to Shanghai and then out of China, thank the Lord,' said Mandy, raising her hands to the sky in prayer. I asked whether they would be returning home.

'No,' said Tina, rummaging inside the big case. 'We're flying to Malaysia … Mandy, where's the spare lock for the air mattress bag?'

'We have to be a little careful there,' she added, her tone growing low and cautious.

'Why?'

'Because it's a Muslim country.' She pronounced the word *moose-lem* and mimed draping a headscarf around her face. 'They're not so keen on our kind there.'

'Oh,' I said, affecting understanding. I hesitated as I chose my next words. 'You mean they … disapprove?'

Mandy's brow furrowed slightly. 'Disapprove?'

Tina paused in the middle of her packing and turned towards me.

'Well, you know,' I said, lowering my tone in line with theirs, 'of your … relationship.'

Mandy's frown deepened. I was suddenly aware of having spoken out of turn—perhaps they wished to keep their sexuality an absolute secret. It was possible, I reasoned, that there really was a husband, or even two, in the background.

'Oh,' I said, affecting an air of vagueness, 'I just mean …
well, you know, they're pretty conservative … generally.'
Mandy continued to stare. I felt my face grow hot. Words
tripped out involuntarily. 'Conservative, you know. About
things like … sleeping arrangements … and whatnot.'

Tina's eyebrows arched in alarm before collapsing into
a look of barely repressed disgust. Drawing herself up, she
said with an affronted, queenly tone, 'We represent the First
National Baptist Church of Madison, Wisconsin. We have
just spent six months spreading the word of Christ throughout Asia. Here,' she said, reaching into the case and handing
me a book. On the cover was an image of a modern church
superimposed with smiling multi-ethnic faces. A text box
proclaimed the word of God in six languages.

'Oh,' I croaked.

'Perhaps you should go now,' said Mandy. 'We won't
need any help with our bags.'

Tina looked at me coldly. 'And I believe these are yours.'
With a deliberate, almost ritualistic motion she held before
my face the glinting blades of my scissors.

Day 4

The last morning. The final wake-up call. The tour guide's
looming presence. She seemed different this morning—
defeated somehow. On her face was none of the malignant
pleasure I associated with her tyrannical reign. Her expression was weary, exhausted almost. The physical depriva-
tions of a tour guide's life aboard the *Lady Water* had taken
their toll. But there was something else, too: an inner,
almost spiritual fatigue, as if, like a dictator who shuts himself in a private room of his palace and cries for some lost

childhood happiness, the effort of maintaining her authoritarian façade had taken with it part of her soul.

'You must wake up,' she said, but her tone was robotic, passionless. She too was a prisoner of the *Lady Water*. 'Wake up, now.'

Mr Snack, on the other hand, bounded out of bed with his usual energy. The polite bow in white slippers was followed by the familiar hawking and spitting. A quick change into grey slacks and electric blue jacket followed. It was the same outfit he had worn at departure, a sartorial bookend to our journey. While I changed he simply sat on his bed like a guru awaiting consultation, hands on knees, silent, straight-backed.

With my packing complete there seemed nothing left to do but wait. For a moment we sat on our beds, facing one another. The atmosphere was calm but oddly expectant: two medieval warriors in the moment before battle, respectful of each other's skills but mindful we would soon be forced to fight to the death. I gave a little bow of my head, a reverent genuflection I might have absorbed from kung fu movies. Mr Snack returned the gesture before beginning a final almighty hawking session, ending with a single green teardrop in the wastepaper bin—a gauntlet thrown down between us.

The engines began to throb and rattle. As the *Lady Water* moved through the dark, closer to the dock, there was another thump on the door. It was the tour guide again. An incomprehensible administrative process followed: we were forced to hand over our room keys in exchange for a receipt with no apparent purpose. As she stomped out the door, I examined my receipt and wished silently for her downfall.

Mr Snack began to gather his bags. The mountains of luggage were too much for one man. With only my backpack weighing me down, I grabbed a couple of cases. Mr Snack looked at me with something close to alarm, but gave a nod of grateful assent.

In the corridors the passengers were milling about in anticipation. As the boat bumped the dock, the chandelier chimed an angry percussion. With the ramps in place, there was the usual fevered rush to disembark; the only difference being that, this time, the desperation was entirely justified.

Down the corridor, Mr Snack and I followed the crowds. As we headed towards the exit I bid joyful goodbyes. Goodbye to the dining room and karaoke lounge. Farewell to the foyer. So long to the canteen gorgons and the tyrannical tour guide. Adios to the passengers, their baseball caps and video cameras. Adieu to the damp, dirt and decrepitude. Later, *Lady Water*.

At the dock a number of other boats were moored. From them streams of people flowed, luggage in tow. On the road beyond, dozens of buses waited, headlights making bars in the fog. Flags in hand, the tour guides marshalled passengers, directing them to buses that would take them to various destinations. I fingered the ticket in my top pocket, fearing, like a hostage released after years in captivity who waits for a bullet in the back, that this might be too good to be true.

We forced our way through the crowds and along the wet road, Mr Snack in front. When we reached his bus, I elbowed others out of the way and heaved his bags into the luggage hold. As he struggled with his final case, I stooped down and threw that, too, into the bus. With an almost shame-faced expression, he nodded briskly.

'Sarnk you,' he said.

I reeled back, dumbfounded. It was as if a suit of armour had come alive or a pet dog announced it wished from now on to sit at the table. In a single moment the irritations of the previous days—rustling packets, drying socks, blaring television and endless phlegm excavations—seemed to disappear, replaced with a sensation best characterised as a sort of melancholy sharpened by unexpected pangs of regret. Mr Snack, at best a curiosity, at worst an irritant, suddenly seemed a sympathetic figure: a lonely man aboard a leaky barge forced into the company of an indifferent stranger. It occurred to me that I had made no effort to bridge the gap between us. Now it was too late. Never would I discover where Mr Snack had come from or where he would go—his dreams and ambitions would remain as much of a mystery as the reasons for his forlorn holiday. As with deliberate, weary motions he gathered the plastic bags of food for the three-hour journey that lay ahead, I could only imagine what might have been.

The tour guide stood by the door of the bus. As she waved passengers aboard, her megaphone, tied with a cord about her neck, beat against her chest. A small commotion among the crowd announced the arrival of a woman, pushing her way through the throngs with the determination of a spawning salmon. Middle-aged and wearing the uniform of the better class of passenger—pleated velvet pants, fluffy sweater with vinyl bands—her forceful entrance only doubled my alarm as I realised she was coming my way.

On small, scissoring legs she pushed past with a practised elbow to my hip. Extending her stout powerful forearms, she began gathering Mr Snack's plastic bags. The two spoke loudly with obvious familiarity. Burdened with their parcels, the pair made their way aboard. The tour guide, taking a break from her incantations, stood aside to allow them entry and acknowledged them with a brief greeting.

'He has found a girlfriend,' I said, sending her an imploring smile. It was a gesture of truce, an acknowledgement that for all our differences we had shared something. There was no point in leaving on bad terms.

'He's wife,' she said simply.

I took a moment to digest this information. 'His wife?'

'Yes,' she said with a note of withering disapproval. 'I tell you. There was mistake. He need bed.'

As the crowds gathered, the tour guide returned to her herding duties. Images came to me as a black-and-white montage, the final revelatory moments of a film noir: buying the ticket from Ronald McDonald; the girl in Chongqing and her urgent getaway; Mr Snack sitting in stoic isolation on the observation deck; his excessive piles of luggage, monstrous mounds of food and resentful silence.

From hidden recesses, dozens of questions launched a ninja surprise attack. Had his wife been on the boat or had I forced her to take another? Had the bed even been mine or had it all been a scam from the start? Was there a berth with my name on it out there, somewhere, on a four-star cruiser equipped with sun deck, full American breakfast and hairdryer sockets? Answers to all this and more would remain forever a mystery. By now the tour guide had climbed aboard and the doors of the bus closed. For a moment I peered frantically through the windows, hopeful of seeing … what, I'm not sure. Mr Snack and his wife had disappeared. Standing at the front the tour guide barked instructions to the passengers. The look on her face was empty, her motions robotic.

On board my bus, there were no familiar faces. Through the window I could see the Irish brothers in a neighbouring vehicle: Liam engrossed in a book, Fintan sprawled against the window, his hair a blond web against the dewy glass.

I was the last passenger. The only seat available was in the furthest back corner. With no room left in storage I balanced my backpack on my lap, my knees pushed hard against the seat in front. Exhausted, I watched the last of the buses pull away as the first light of morning revealed spindly black trees in the grey.

All at once exhaustion overcame me. Gently, my face fell against my pack, scratchy but soft. As I closed my eyes a profound restfulness embraced me. It was the sleep of days, of 3 a.m. temple hikes, of an overwhelming gratitude for having finally left the *Lady Water*.

Lost in a daze, the first jab in my ribs seemed a dream. The second opened my eyes, bringing me face to face with the bus driver and a dozen half-curious, half-accusing eyes. The driver leaned in. He pointed to a ticket in his hand. I knew the words before he spoke them.

'You must pay!'

Bollywood Nights

Mumbai is the kind of town where you can buy a poster of an eight-armed woman eating a baby then give your change to a no-armed man eating a mango with his feet. In a city where anything is possible—except renting a home, finding a public toilet or driving a car—becoming a movie star can seem pretty unremarkable.

Mumbai is a city of serendipity. It couldn't be otherwise. Like a volatile chemical brew crammed full of excited molecules, things happen in this town: people bump into one another, strange phenomena occur, in an instant the ordinary becomes extraordinary and you are vaulted from the everyday to the realm of magic. That I might be spotted to star in a film on my first day in town did not, therefore, seem that weird. In fact, in a city where weird is normal and bizarre is merely mildly diverting, it barely raises an eyebrow.

The spotter's name was Mahesh. As it happened I didn't ring him until, with happy symmetry, my final day in the country. By then the initial nerve-shattering shock I had felt upon arrival in India had settled into a mild but constant panic, like the low ringing of a distant fire alarm that you have almost become accustomed to. During this time I had discovered that approaches to westerners to be extras in films were a regular feature of life in Mumbai and not, disappointingly, due to any special charisma I might have exuded. Regardless, Mahesh was happy to hear from me.

'Oh, Mr Brendan. Of course I am remembering. Please, be meeting me this evening. We are needing a doctor.'

'Oh no—is something wrong?'

'No, no. You, *you* are being a doctor.'

I arrived at the arranged spot that evening. On the pavement outside Leopold's Cafe stood a group of three foreigners, two girls and a boy, all very young. Before I could introduce myself, I felt a pressure on my arm. 'Come,' said Mahesh, dragging me away. 'We are being very late.'

In the cab on our way to the train station I got to know the others. Adele was Dutch but spoke English with an aristocratic accent so refined I found it difficult to believe it wasn't her first language. She was quieter than her friend, a touch chubby and sullen. Victoria was Zimbabwean but had lived all over the world. She was thin and twitchy with the strident manner of a head nurse or one of those pissed-off women behind Perspex at one of the more hellish government agencies, immigration per-haps. The girls were travelling together and had been in India many months.

The boy, Bertrand, was only eighteen. Spotty and pudgy with no chin and a floppy blond fringe, he looked like the kind of posh Englishman last seen going off to lick the Hun before dying in a hail of bullets atop a string of razor wire to the tune of 'Jerusalem'. He was travelling in India until he could begin his degree at Oxford. He had been away only a week and was already determined to go home.

'My girlfriend really wants to see me,' he said mournfully.

'You can't leave India for a girl,' said Victoria.

'Hmm,' said Bertrand. 'But you see I also have this terrible …' He leaned in and lowered his voice: '… diarrhoea.'

'Oh, God!' boomed Victoria. '*Everyone* in India has fucking diarrhoea. What makes you special?'

Shit is to travellers in India what the weather is to the English—the subject everyone can agree on. Anyone who has been in the country for any time has some horror story about a close call, near miss or spectacular blowout that will haunt them forever. In India every fart is Russian roulette, every stomach grumble a finger poised above the red button of anal Armageddon. It's a great social leveller, so it doesn't take long for people to start trading war stories.

As someone who can quite happily give minute-by-minute updates on the fluctuations of my bowels, this is fine by me. Scatological is not a dirty word in my vocabulary. In fact I take a perverse pride in collecting the best diarrhoea stories. If you think this is weird or distasteful, then I can only assume you haven't been to India. If you have, then I can only assume you were some sort of high-ranking dignitary who brought their own supply of food and drinking water. Too bad. You missed out on some very good stories.

We arrived at the vast neo-Gothic building that is Victoria Terminus. Inside, Mahesh bought tickets while we waited on the platform and let the rivers of humanity flow about us. The arrival of our train signalled a panicked rush for the door, panic being the only way to approach Indian transport.

The trains in Mumbai are hell—every time I catch one I expect to see a big sign at my destination saying ARBEIT MACHT FREI. The carriages are filthy. The few seats are covered in a green plastic that clings to your thighs, mingling your sweat with that of countless thousands of others. The walls are a tangle of steel reinforcements and wire mesh, the windows cracked or smashed by missiles thrown by slum children—people avoid sitting next to them for fear of taking a brick to the head. Despite the oppressive heat there is no air conditioning. Instead, hundreds of steel fans in grime-caked cages whir viciously, inches from your face. At night the carriages are starkly lit by neon tubes connected by gnarled tendrils of wiring that occasionally arc and fizz to rain small showers of sparks on alarmed passengers.

The trains themselves are only half the horror of Mumbai transit. The crowds are the worst in the world, in both their numbers and conduct. Coaches are often so packed you physically cannot get out at your stop, forcing you to wait until there have been enough stops to clear the carriage. After this you must fight your way through the sweating bodies and cross to the other side of the platform to take a train in the opposite direction. Of course, there is no guarantee your return journey will be any less crowded. I am convinced that at any one time in Mumbai there are thousands of people stuck in an endless circle of trains and platforms, struggling futilely against an immobile mass of people.

The etiquette of Indian train commuters is totally free of Anglo restraint, feigned or otherwise. There are no studied expressions of disinterest as you try to find a seat, no subtle attempts to angle your way in front of the guy next to you, no resigned, bovine shuffles into the carriage. On Mumbai trains people sprint for seats with a reckless self-ishness that would shame even New Yorkers. That evening I stared, dumbfounded, as a small man in a turban ran into the carriage, moving his arms backwards in a karate-chop motion, hitting passengers behind him in the chest and throat.

The demurely titled 'Ladies Only' coaches are havens from the constant sexual harassment an unaccompanied woman can expect to suffer in the regular carriages but offer few other compensations. With their bench seats and bare wooden floors they verge on cattle trucks. To get inside, housewives gather their saris about themselves, take a short run then fling themselves deep into the mass of bodies. That night I watched with scepticism as a hefty woman in bright red silk slammed into an entrance so tightly packed it was impossible to tell which limb belonged to which body. To my surprise, and seemingly in defiance of the laws of physics, she slowly disappeared into the human wall, like a cherry sinking into custard.

By the time we approached the station nearest the studio it was getting late and Victoria was growing increasingly moody. 'Mahesh,' she demanded, 'do you promise we'll be out of this thing by 2 a.m.?'

Mahesh wobbled his head in a reassuring manner.

'What does that mean?'

He just wobbled his head again, more softly this time.

The girls, it turned out, were Bollywood veterans. They had been in a dozen films and funded their accommodation with appearances.

'We were supposed to be in one yesterday,' said Adele, 'but the shoot fell through. It was a pity because were supposed to be diving into a pool during a dance sequence. We were going to make a thousand rupees for that.'

Up until now, I had not considered the issue of payment. The idea that we would be paid—and no small amount, by Indian standards—for what millions would gladly do for free, simply because we had white faces, struck me as both marvellous and rather unfair. Yet, as is common in India, I didn't have long to contemplate the injustice. As soon as we stepped off the train we were immediately plunged into a maelstrom of humanity. Mahesh ran ahead, reminding us, like the White Rabbit, we were running late. It was an effort to keep up as I fought my way through hawkers brandishing every conceivable type of good, service or physical deformity.

The persistence of Indian salesmen and shopkeepers is legendary. The term 'just browsing' has no meaning here. It is only ever assumed you are in the market for anything: from a bag of cashews to a jumbo tub of skin lotion, from a mechanical toy to a pirated DVD, from a novelty belt buckle to a religious icon. As I elbowed past a knife grinder and a man selling windmill toys, a woman thrust three freshly slaughtered chickens in my face. As she waggled the bloodied carcasses, their slashed throats opened and closed like dreadful little mouths.

The studio was a small, shabby affair just near the border of Film City, a village of studios that is the heart of the Indian film industry. A thick fog of pollution had settled in the area and there was a nauseating smell of burning plastic. Gathered around the concrete walls of the studio were mounds of discarded plastic cups and a vocal fraternity of drunken taxi drivers. The wall served as their combined bar and urinal and the stench of piss was overwhelming.

Mahesh banged on a wooden door within enormous steel gates. A small man appeared to usher us inside and the door slammed behind us. Bisecting the grounds of the studio was a fake streetscape lined with old-fashioned electric lamps. To one side stood a colonial post office; on the other were some modern blocks of studios. A pack of barrel-ribbed dogs prowled the streetscape. One sniffed half-heartedly at my feet before turning to piss on a lamppost. In the weird half-light of the pollution it could have been the final, melancholy scene of a forgotten silent comedy.

After Mahesh's constant haranguing it was frustrating to discover that we seemed to be early. In the best tradition of filmmaking, we sat down and waited.

Movie sets are always eerie, but in India especially so. In the subcontinent you find yourself in an almost constant state of alert—after only a few weeks of fending off every kind of approach, scam and hassle, you acquire the nerves of a ninja, ready to snap a man's neck before disappearing silently up a tree. After ten minutes of being left to your own devices, unmolested by anyone forcing upon you a trinket, sob story or incurable disease, you begin to grow oddly anxious. Bertrand pointed to the post office. 'That must be the only veranda in India that doesn't have someone sleeping on it.'

Victoria and Adele drifted off to chat with someone they recognised from a previous shoot. Bertrand and I, meanwhile, sat slapping mosquitoes and feeling bored and disappointed. Our tedium was relieved by the arrival of a man clutching a pair of uniforms. 'Here,' he said, thrusting a blue outfit and cap at us both.

I turned the cap over to examine a disarmingly realistic British police insignia. Any disappointment I might have felt at not being a doctor was immediately forgotten. I could scarcely contain my excitement: I was to be a cop in a movie.

Like foiling a hijacking, shooting a trench full of Nazis or becoming a professional stunt driver, being a movie cop is a macho fantasy I have entertained for much of my life but which weakness, both physical and mental, has forced me to supress. I couldn't believe my luck. I began to consider my character. How would he draw his gun? How would he kick in a door—foot straight up or side on with a twist, karate-style? Would he have smartarse one-liners? Perhaps something appropriate to the Indian setting: 'Meet my old friend, Mahatma Gun-di,' or, 'I'm gonna kick your Maha-butt-ara.'

All at once, I was struck by a horrible thought. I put my hand to my face—after six weeks in India I looked like a mall Santa. 'I have a beard!' I said to the casting director, pointing to the thing as though it were the first symptom of a new disease.

He frowned in confusion. 'Yes,' he said.

'No, no,' I said, attempting to clarify. 'Policemen don't have beards.' He stared at me blankly. 'I'll shave it off,' I said, miming the action.

Without a word, but with a look that might have been disgust, he turned and walked back inside.

Despondently I changed into the uniform then made my way to the shoot, convinced that the director would take one look at me and immediately call for a replacement. In my surprisingly well-fitting, albeit reeking, pants I hovered behind the cameras, cap in hand, and watched the filming.

The room was small, very hot and full of mosquitoes. The make-up woman continually mopped the faces of the two male leads before re-dusting them with powder until a white tidemark began to cake their brow lines. There were two other guys playing 'English' cops. Time and again they walked through a pair of saloon doors while the leads attempted to remember their lines. As I watched them my fears of rejection were soon quelled. One was unmistakably German, immensely tall and grave with a large nest of dreadlocks rolled under his hat; the other a Belgian raver with bleached blond hair and a silver hoop earring the size of pickle lid in either ear.

For half an hour I stood watching, not knowing what to do. Occasionally I made subtle enquiries regarding my role but was met only with stony indifference by a harassed crew. Finally a cut was called. I readied to take my place in the spotlight. To my dismay, the director, an unusually tall, stooped man with a hangdog expression, gave an order in Hindi and the crew began to dismantle the set. Like a bride stood up at the altar I looked around mournfully, hoping this was not as final as it seemed. In desperation I grabbed the German policeman. 'What's going on?' I asked.

'Zis is all cray-see,' he said, pulling off his hat and allowing the dreadlocks to cascade down his back.

Filled with indignation I marched outside, where I spied the man who'd given me the uniform. 'When do I get to act?' I asked accusingly.

'What are you doing!' he said in a crisp English accent. 'Get out of that costume and change back into your clothes. They're waiting for you up there.' He pointed to the second storey of one of the studio buildings. He acted as if I should have known the entire thing had been moved.

'By the way,' I said, 'what is this movie called?'

'Talk to the director,' he said and strode off.

'Is that the name of the movie or an instruction?' I was being smart, but I don't think he heard me.

Upstairs I joined the girls and Bertrand, who were pushing one another across the room on wheeled office chairs while set builders worked at the other end, painting Royal Bank of Scotland signs on the windows. Once more it seemed I was rushing to nowhere.

By now it was getting late. Our prospects of leaving before 2 a.m. were looking slim. The others were getting hungry and whiny.

'I want some food,' said Bertrand, rubbing his tummy like Winnie-the-Pooh.

'I thought you had diarrhoea,' I said.

'I do,' he replied glumly.

A short while later Mahesh tapped me on the shoulder. 'Come, Brendan. We are eating.'

'Oh *goody*,' said Bertrand.

Downstairs in a smoky shed the caterers had prepared a buffet of steaming witches' cauldrons. We loaded our plates and squatted in the dust to eat an assortment of surprisingly excellent curries and dhals. The relatively pleasant atmosphere was soon shattered, however, by the outbreak of a savage dog fight at the centre of our group. As it grew in intensity, Victoria became distressed. 'Can't somebody do something?' she screamed.

Two large dogs held down a smaller one, not much bigger than a pup. It whimpered and yelped as they chomped at its neck and head. Nobody did anything. Like me they were either too scared to get involved with these semi-wild animals, or—as was possible in a nation of vegetarians who are apparently unsentimental about animals—they simply didn't care.

As the dogs savaged the whimpering pup, Victoria began to sob quietly. Adele made an effort to comfort her. On the other side of the shed I heard the guy with the dhal bucket say to Bertrand, 'No, I told you—there isn't any more.'

Dinner finished, we returned to the building, where we were asked to wait in a distant room decked out as a corporate office. The Indian concept of what the inner sanctum of a 'powerful businessman' ought to look like was telling: Dr Evil's headquarters at the heart of his volcano lair except with holes punched in the walls, Wedgewood shepherdess figurines on the bookcase and a series of light boxes stuck about the room featuring blurry pictures of men in suits overlaid with text saying things like, 'computer!', 'information age!' and 'bussiness!' I still had no idea what I was doing or when we would be starting.

'I'm thirsty,' whined Bertrand.

Sitting in an office chair, Victoria kicked off the wall and rolled across the room. 'Fucking cunts,' she muttered. 'What do any of them care? What if it was *their* dog?'

A group of Indian extras who had arrived after dinner looked up and shot one another nervous glances.

Eventually Mahesh popped his head into the room. 'Hey, guys! Please be looking sharpish.'

Following him into the other half of the studio I was astonished to find it had been transformed into a passable reproduction of a Scottish bank, complete with accurate corporate logos and an unnerving northern spring light flooding through the windows. It was all held together with electrical tape and looked as if it might collapse at any second, but it was far more convincing than anticipated.

A woman with a clipboard directed us towards various desks around the set. 'Excuse me,' I said, 'but what is this film called?' She just shrugged and walked away.

Lounging behind my desk I fiddled with the stapler and tried to make conversation with the girl seated beside me. She was Indian and when I asked if she often did work as an extra she arched her back, flicked her hair over her shoulders and said, '*I* am an actress.'

It was difficult not to notice that an uncomfortable apartheid had developed between the western and Indian extras. The latter made no effort to speak to us and any attempt to approach them was met with cold indifference. At first I thought they couldn't speak English, until I realised they spoke it among themselves. In the end, the only conclusion I could come to was that they hated us.

To a degree, I understood why. In India, movies are a serious business. Not just in terms of serious money and serious fame; they are cherished more dearly than anyone who grew up eating popcorn at multiplexes can comprehend. When you live in a house made of cow shit and your ambition in life is to live past puberty, escapism isn't escapism: it's all you have.

By being in the movies in India you achieve a level of fame for which there is no comparison in the west. Stars are worshipped as gods—literally. For several years, the West Bengal chapter of the fan club for Amitabh Bachchan, India's biggest star, has been raising funds to build a giant marble temple dedicated to him. In some personal shrines, especially in southern India, it is not unheard of to find pictures of Bachchan and others stuck beside those of favourite gods. When he was injured during a shoot in the 1980s, a hundred thousand people rioted at his hospital and one man ran 550 kilometres backwards as an offering to the gods to ensure his recovery.

It makes waiting twelve hours at the Oscar red carpet look pretty tame and the thought occurred to me that I was not, perhaps, treating this evening's excursions with enough seriousness. Hollywood might seem competitive but compared to India, where a billion people were going for the role of third bank teller from the left, it looked like an open casting call for the role of a leaflet guy in a hotdog costume. The Indian extras weren't just kids doing it for some extra cash and a plate of lentils; they were actually trying to 'make it'. I couldn't blame them for resenting us.

Then again, as I looked about the room at the portly girls fixing their make-up, geeky guys in tight pants and the sad old man who looked as if he'd been wheeled in without consent from some nearby palliative ward, I couldn't help but think that aspiring Indian actors were just as delusional as their western counterparts.

Before we knew it, the movie was happening. Two guys in gorilla masks clutching guns stood about doing a script run-through with the director while a pretty girl with big black hair and a substantial belly hanging out of her crop top 'emoted' in a corner.

The floodlights came on and people began to ready themselves. The director moved around the room, barking orders. I turned to the actress beside me. 'What are we supposed to do?' I asked. She exhaled impatiently and explained that the guys in the masks were going to rob us and that I had to get down on my knees with my hands up, looking terrified. This I had not been counting on. When I'd accepted this job I had pictured myself in the background somewhere, typing at a computer or clutching a cocktail. The idea of actually acting filled me with apprehension. In one night I had gone from being a doctor to a cop to a frightened bank teller and my motivation was starting to get hazy.

In the centre of the room, the female lead stared condescendingly at everyone as the make-up woman fluffed her hair. 'Is she famous?' I asked the girl beside me.

'Hmph. I have never before seen her.'

I pointed to the script on her desk. 'Hey,' I said, 'do you know what this movie is called?' She held up the title page but it was in Hindi. 'I can't read Hindi,' I said. She smiled smugly.

The director began shouting. There was a scramble by cast and crew. The filming went so quickly I assumed it was a rehearsal. The bank robbers in monkey masks burst onto the set, forcing us all to our knees. I complied, trembling and quivering. A cut was called and they started the scene with the heroine. Creeping up behind her, the robbers held a gun to her head. In the scene's central gag she was too busy speaking on her mobile phone to notice. She tried to make the most of the slapstick possibilities of her role but, to be fair, there was only so much you could do and still be sure the set would stay standing.

Watching the actress ham her way through her lines I was reminded of the tacky stories I had read in the Mumbai press. They always started with the words 'Bollywood starlet' and ended in a lurid description of the discovery of a body in a canal. Suspicious circumstances were soon ruled out, suicide notes and grieving mothers produced, but dark implications remained. Questions about Starlet X who had last been seen with Producer Y at a 'notorious gangster' haunt were raised. The story would last two days before everyone forgot about the girl from Uttar Pradesh who came to Bollywood to make it big but ended up running with wrong crowd. At least, I thought, I now have a face to put to the name.

Two takes, a quick look at the playback and that was it. All over. Have a cup of tea. Go home. The incongruous spring lights were switched off and the windows went dark, leaving us once more in a dilapidated office block in suburban Mumbai.

I had done my work admirably. In fact, I had been the only extra with a close-up. Any ironic distance I might have had from the Bollywood experience had been replaced with genuine excitement, as if it were only a matter of time before a producer watching a rough cut pulled a cigar from his mouth and said, 'Him! I want that boy. Let's make him a star.' And why not? This was Mumbai after all. Stranger things had happened here.

Still high from the experience of my first role, I chatted with the others as we pulled the skin of fat from the top of our chai. It was relatively early, 2.30 a.m., and everyone was pleased. Few people seemed to be left. The actress who had sat beside me was nowhere to be seen. Nor, for that matter, were any of the rest of the Indian cast. I wondered how they had left so quickly without me noticing. I imagined the actress, the old man and the boys in tight slacks waiting out front, an unlikely union mob, tapping billy clubs in their hands, ready to give us a beat down.

'And for you,' said Mahesh, handing me a 500-rupee note.

'What is this movie called?' I asked.

'Hah! I don't know.' Mahesh laughed. 'Nobody here is knowing anything!'

Out on the street the taxi drivers had gone. Only a pile of empty bottles of homemade whisky and the whiff of piss remained, less sour now in the morning air. While we waited by the side of the road Mahesh stood in the middle, madly waving at approaching vehicles. In the mist their headlights were solid bars of white. Victoria yawned and Adele rubbed her back. Finally a cab was flagged down and we all piled in: me in front, sitting on Mahesh's lap, bent double, my face resting on the window ledge. My memory of Mumbai at this time of night is always the same: grey concrete tenements, highway overpasses and endless homes of tin and cardboard, their residents sleeping in rows in the dust.

As we approached downtown a cart driven by an old man suddenly appeared. It was a plain cart, the tray full of firewood. The bulls pulling it were enormous, their horns the length of pool cues. Their entire bodies, tip to tip, were painted bright pink. On their flanks were drawn many crimson swastikas.

Excitedly, I turned to the others. In the back, Victoria and Adele were slumped against one another asleep. Bernard, meanwhile, lay with his face squished against the window, drool making snail trails down the glass. Underneath me, Mahesh had folded his arms and dropped his head back onto the seat. The scene was all mine to enjoy.

As we passed the bulls, the cart driver met my eyes and flicked his whip at their massive backs. It was a fantastic sight, a spectacle bigger than cinema and stranger than fiction. Another moment of joyful serendipity in the city of chances.

A Grand Gesture

It's surprising how cold Flagstaff, Arizona, can be in winter, especially at night, especially if you're wearing nothing but underpants and a coat. Even more surprising is how warm piss can be. As I walked through the knee-high snow, drops fell regularly from the soaking bag, a line of tiny steaming holes marking my trail, as if I were being continually shot at but missed by a weak laser beam.

In reception all was dark and silent. A bearded hippy lay sleeping, face down on the desk under the beam of a reading lamp, his hand outstretched, holding an invisible pen. I roused him with a shake to the shoulder. 'Excuse me,' I said. 'I need some help.'

Slowly, he sat up, still stuck in his flattened posture. In the lamplight, a string of saliva spun a delicate silken thread between the desk and his mouth.

'Excuse me,' I said. 'I need a trash bag. Do you have one?' The hippy made a noise, something between a wet gurgle and a questioning exclamation. His head turned in my direction but his eyes stayed closed. I repeated my question.

Running a hand down his face he opened his eyes. Black hair painted delicate arabesques across his cheek. 'Huh?'

I repeated myself again.

'Oh *yeah*,' said the hippy, as if he had any idea what I was talking about.

'Yes,' I said. 'A plastic trash bag, please. If you have one.'

The hippy nodded. 'Oh, a *bag*,' he said, as if he had suddenly remembered what it was: the crinkly black thing, great for holding garbage, can be tied at the top. 'Oh yeah, a bag, man,' he said, as if the word held some musical or talismanic property, as if 'bag' might have been code for something else, something that could not be said openly: an ounce of weed or twenty carats of stolen diamonds, perhaps. 'Yeah, dude. A *bag*.' He began to rummage behind the desk, opening drawers and cupboards, then slamming them shut. 'A bag,' he repeated to himself.

Suddenly, he stopped and turned, his tired eyes full of genuine but aggravating, hippyish concern. 'Hey, dude,' he said. 'How come you *need* a bag?'

***

A few hours' drive north of Phoenix, Flagstaff is one of those slightly self-satisfied American college towns full of the sort of people who bring guitars to parties. I had arrived the previous afternoon, drawn, like many other casual visitors, by the town's proximity to the Grand Canyon. I was due to visit in the morning but right now Flagstaff was just a bed to me, a place to sleep off the migraine that had been threatening to flower for the last hour. As I checked into the hostel, a disco ball of migraine lights was just beginning to spin behind my eyes.

A man smelling of something between camp fire and hotdog water showed me to my dorm. 'Here it is, dude,' he said. 'You got it all to yourself.' He gestured to the empty bunk beds and smiled as if I were Little Orphan Annie and he my Daddy Warbucks, revealing a world of previously unimagined luxury.

Crawling into bed, I took two of my migraine tablets and pulled a pillow over my head, preparing to ride out the pain I knew would soon hit me like a cartoon safe dropping from the sky.

Contrary to what many believe, a migraine isn't just a bad headache, it's a state of altered consciousness, a trip down a rabbit hole of pain. A migraine is its own little dimension with its own rules and logic. People with migraines don't walk around the office, rubbing their temples and saying, 'I have a migraine,' because people with migraines don't walk or talk or do anything else; they lie down and suffer and wait because that's all they can do.

As the migraine peaked, time became relative. Minutes felt like hours, hours became days. I forgot where I was then remembered then forgot again. As it passed I fell into a deep drug-induced sleep broken only by strange, vivid dreams. In one I was travelling through a landscape of saguaro cacti with human faces. On the Greyhound was the Native American guy who had sat beside me from Phoenix, smoking pot. 'Look, the saguaro are waving,' he said. Out the window the cacti smiled and flopped their adorable chubby cactus arms in greeting. 'And now it's raining,' he said, and the landscape was gone, replaced by a strange new scene.

The image was so vivid as to seem unreal—a perfectly rendered, billion-pixel computer graphic. Against a dark backdrop the torso of a naked man stood holding his pale flaccid penis. From it gushed a heavy stream of urine, arcing downwards and landing with some force in my backpack.

I cannot remember the precise moment I realised this was not a dream. Perhaps it was when the first fine spray of piss hit my face, or the smell, rich in the particular tang of an overworked liver.

I sprang upright in bed. 'What are you doing?' I screamed.

With the benefit of hindsight this question would come to seem rather stupid. It was, after all, perfectly obvious what he was doing—he was pissing in my backpack. What I really should have asked was: 'Why are you doing this?' Although that, too, was obvious—he was out of his mind with booze. Perhaps a more pertinent question might have been, 'Who are you?' Although that didn't really matter either. He might have been a former astronaut or the star of a minor sitcom and he would still be the guy pissing in my backpack.

I pushed him hard. Loops and arcs of urine splashed across the floor and wall as he stumbled. 'Hey, watch it!' he cried in an aggrieved tone, as if I had done something entirely unreasonable: shoved past him on the subway escalator or spilled a hot drink in his lap. With unsteady steps he made his way to the bathroom, leaving a wet trail behind him. 'I'll get you those tin cans in the morning,' he called over the noise of his seemingly unending stream slapping the tiled floor.

Still in a state of shock, I inspected my backpack. On top sat my smaller day pack. In it were the usual things you might associate with a day of sightseeing: a bottle of water, a guidebook, some chocolate-chip cookies and a packet of dried apricots. None of it exactly irreplaceable. Much more worryingly it also contained my camera, a journal with two months of notes, my migraine medication and, this being the pre-digital era, a Walkman accompanied by approximately twenty lovingly crafted mix tapes. More important than all this, however, was the traveller's holy of holies: my money belt. In it was my entire existence, my lifeline, my ejector seat, the piece of string leading back to the entrance of the Minotaur's labyrinth. It contained my passport, $2000 in US traveller's cheques, $500 in cash, my vaccination card, insurance policy and return ticket (this being a time when people were still using paper tickets and airlines treated them as if they were hand-illuminated medieval Bibles and took immense and spiteful satisfaction in forcing you to pay absurd amounts to print replacements).

I pulled out the dripping day pack. Under it half my clothes were soaked. From the bathroom I could still hear my roommate mumbling and knocking things over. I thought for a moment then pulled on my overcoat, slipped my feet into my boots, opened the door and made my way into the snow.

The hippy had finally found a garbage bag. As I kneeled on the floor, peeling apart my documents, he sympathised. 'Oh, that's Dave, man,' he said. 'Dave's a great guy but when he gets drunk he does crazy things. That is totally uncool of Dave, man.'

Uncool? Yes, that was one word for it. Although 'uncool' was, to my mind, wearing your Star Trek costume on a date or having a tattoo of your name in Chinese characters on your lower back. Urinating on someone's worldly possessions is more something a violent sadist does to his new prison cellmate to prepare him for a new life of sexual and financial servitude.

Into the garbage bag I threw everything that wasn't absolutely necessary. Out went the sodden cookies and the apricots. Stacks of old tickets and maps, heavy with piss, joined them. My camera was ruined. Looking into the viewfinder revealed a rocking yellow sea. When I opened the deck of my Walkman a rivulet trickled out and rolled down my arm. My beloved mix tapes were sloshing miniature aquariums. As I threw them into the bag I recalled the hours of rewinding and pausing, the careful curatorship that had gone into their creation, the accreted memories they represented. All of it gone now, like so many sodden cookies.

I took my clothes to the laundry and washed them at the highest possible heat with three cups of detergent. Back in the office, atop another garbage bag, I laid out my essentials. I needed somewhere to leave them to dry, somewhere safe. There was my passport, ticket and more than $2000, but what could I do? I had no choice. I needed to trust the hippy.

'Yeah, no problem, dude,' he said. 'I am, like, so sorry about this. Like I said, Dave's a great guy but this is really uncool of him. I guess we gotta kick him out now. 'Cause this shit is bad, man. Like I said, really uncool.'

It was almost 4 a.m. I wanted a couple of hours' sleep before my journey to the Grand Canyon. The hippy gave me a new room. 'Don't worry, dude. It's all cool. I'll take care of everything and no one will touch your stuff. You have, like, totally, my word.'

I have no idea why I chose to believe him at that point. Though he was, perhaps, not a thief, he was most definitely an idiot. Exhausted and with a migraine hangover, smelling like a downtown bus shelter, still wearing my underwear and overcoat, alone and far from home, I wanted—needed—to believe that there was someone on my side. 'Thanks, dude,' I said and, not knowing what else to do, extended a cold wet hand.

I might have slept but I didn't rest. My fear that I had, essentially, placed my life in the hands of a hippy I had only known an hour, made relaxing impossible. For what seemed an eternity I slipped in and out of consciousness, plagued by images of him running away with my money and identity: the hippy lying in a hammock on a beach in Mexico smoking a joint the size of a telegraph pole; on a shopping spree, buying dream catchers, fire sticks and Burning Man tickets; boarding a plane for Fiji with some woman who looked like Patti Smith and used a sea sponge for a tampon.

At about 6 a.m. I got up.

As I entered the reception a familiar reek of piss hit me. It seemed difficult to believe: how could my bag have caused this? It was if the stench had a life if its own, multiplying like virulent bacteria. Perhaps it was all around me and I had simply grown accustomed to it. I couldn't even imagine how I might smell.

Inside there were a couple of people milling about, waiting for the guide to take us to the Grand Canyon. The hippy was nowhere to be seen but on the front desk I found a note: *Brandon: your stuff is in the safe. Chill. The owner will give it to you when you get back from the Canyon. Stay cool. Peregrine (nite dude).*

Behind the desk was a short, scowling man with a crew cut and a pair of camouflage pants, a miniature drill sergeant. 'Excuse me,' I said, holding up the note. 'Are you the owner?'

For a moment he looked at me. Suddenly a furious scowl fractured his face. 'Are you the one with the bag full of piss?' he said.

'Well … yes.'

'You're fucking disgusting, dude.'

'Ah, excuse me?' I said, confused.

'Excuse me,' he said, mocking my accent. 'Excuse me? Excuse me!' He came out from behind the desk and walked closer. 'No fucking way, asshole! I'm not gonna excuse you. I ain't gonna excuse shit.'

'I'm sorry,' I said. 'What are you talking about?'

'Oh, what am I talking about?' He turned to the others. 'He asks what I'm fucking talking about.' His focus returned to me. 'I'm talking about the goddamn bag full of piss, asshole.'

'What about it?' I said.

'You're fucking disgusting, dude!' he exploded. 'How would you like it? How would you like it if I came over to your house and pissed on your fucking table? Because that's what you've done, asshole. It's like you came in here, dude, and pissed on my fucking table!'

Breathing deeply I gathered my thoughts. I was confused and aggrieved. I wanted to defend myself, to explain that I had been the victim. More importantly, I wanted my money and passport, but there seemed little I could do. This guy was obviously not going to give me anything. All I had to hold onto was the reassurances of a man named after a bird who couldn't spell 'night'.

'Look, I'm not quite sure what you're talking about,' I said. 'But I don't care either way. I've had a really bad night. So I'm going to go to the Grand Canyon and when I come back I'm getting my stuff and then I'm getting outta here, okay?'

'Oh, is that right?' he retorted. 'Well you better not even fucking *think* about coming back here, asshole.'

The guide had arrived by now and the others had climbed into the minivan. As I went outside to join them, the drill sergeant stuck his head out the front door.

'Disgusting, dude. Fucking disgusting is what you are.'

***

Trying to describe the Grand Canyon is futile: like asking an ant to describe a picnic from the edge of a bowl of potato salad. There is nothing to compare it to, nothing in your experience you can say it is like. It is so enormous as to be almost implausible. Seeing it from the lookouts of the South Rim you might as well be watching a three-dimensional tourist film of the Grand Canyon: at any minute I expected to hear a narrator say, 'The majestic Grand Canyon, truly one of nature's wonders,' before the scene disappeared, the lights went on and we all filed out through the gift shop.

To get a better sense of its scale, I tried to hike down at least part of the way. On an icy path I slipped and landed on my backside, sliding to a precarious halt at the edge of a sheer cliff. Giving up, I returned to the top, feeling the frozen mud turn to water and ruin my only pants not soaked in urine. When I went to get something to eat I realised I had no money, my wallet having also been in the bag and now in the safe or, quite possibly, the hippy's threadbare pocket. Reduced to begging from some fellow travellers I sat on a bench, shivering, and ate a lunch of a sour orange, some rice cakes and a fistful of trail mix. All that was missing was a crack of thunder coming from a little cartoon raincloud over my head.

By the time we got back to the hostel it was dark. My anxiety about my possessions was added to a fear of the potential confrontation that awaited. I devised a plan: sneak in, grab my stuff and get out again. The question of where I would sleep would have to be answered later.

Cautiously I made my way inside. To my surprise, there was a small party underway. A handful of new guests were drinking cheap red wine and listening to music. It still smelled of piss.

I looked for the owner. No one seemed to know who or where he might be. I imagined the hippy smiling to himself as he followed the Grateful Dead in a newly purchased methane-powered van. I began to grow frantic, searching the corridors of the hostel. As I rounded a corner, the eyes of the drill sergeant met mine. He set a collision course. I held up my hands defensively, but he paid no attention. 'I gotta talk to you, dude,' he said, coming closer.

'Sorry,' I said. 'I'm getting my stuff and leaving.'

'This is for you.' He handed me a plastic bag. Inside was my passport, money and everything else. All of it was bone dry, albeit it with a telltale yellow tinge. I fingered the traveller's cheques disbelievingly, as if they might have been forgeries. The drill sergeant stared at me, his cropped hair amplifying the craziness of his green eyes. He stuck a finger in my face. 'You taught me today, dude. You taught me something I will never fucking forget.'

His tone was as aggressive as it had been in the morning, making it impossible to tell what he was referring to or where this might be leading. 'What's that?' I said.

'You fucking *taught* me, dude.'

I braced myself for a punch or roundhouse karate kick to the stomach.

'You taught me HUMILITY! I have been *humbled* by you, dude. I am *ashamed* of myself.' The word 'ashamed' was delivered with the same ferocity with which he had called me an asshole, so it took a moment to realise he seemed to be making some kind of apology.

'Dude!' he yelled, pointing at me, his eyes drawing very close to mine. 'You are like the fucking Dalai Lama or some shit. How do you fucking *do it*, dude?'

'Do what?' I asked cautiously, still not entirely sure this wasn't some elaborate decoy, a prelude to a knife in the neck.

'Stay so fucking calm, dude! I mean, I'm here getting all up in your face for something you didn't do and you're just taking it, dude. I am a motherfucking *asshole*! That is the goddamn truth and I apologise to you for it, man.' His tone became fractionally quieter, his manner more intense and focused. 'You taught me. You taught me something I will *never* forget. You taught me humility, dude. *Humility*.'

——

It took half an hour to determine what had happened. From a corner of the common room a plastic garbage bag was produced. Inside were all the things I had discarded the previous night. Weirdly, they were all dry but smelled like a crack house mattress. Gagging, I retied the bag and asked why it had not been thrown away. The hippy, as it turned out, had taken his responsibilities towards me more seriously than I could have ever imagined.

Apparently, after I had left him, he had taken the contents of the garbage bag and laid it out on radiators throughout the hostel. Consequently, not only were my passport and money dry, but so were such essential items as a stash of old maps, various Greyhound ticket stubs, my tapes and Walkman, a notebook, a bulging paper bag full of receipts, my migraine medication … even the dried apricots and the squashed packet of chocolate-chip cookies. By dawn the smell had infected the whole place.

My initial reaction was astonishment—astonishment that anyone might have considered, even for a moment, that I would have done anything so stupid. There was a kind of awe, too: what mind had done this? What kind of person would see an outdated LA bus timetable soaked in urine and think: *Well, I'll just dry that off, separate it from that month-old handbill for a punk show and that photocopied map of Tucson, peel the pages apart and it will be right as rain*? I mean: how do you get to the point in life in which a soaking of bodily waste from a homeless degenerate does not mean having to discard an otherwise perfectly edible packet of cookies?

Yet, to my surprise, I was also rather touched. The hippy had not only made good on his promise but had gone above and beyond the call of duty. I imagined him at 4 a.m., gently placing each sodden item on the radiator, leaving a grotesque trail of urine behind him. 'He'll need these,' he might have said as he spread out my tapes or balanced each apricot. It was an incomprehensible gesture, but one of strange tenderness—a cat leaving a mutilated rat on your pillow. It restored my faith in humanity; a modest act in the grand scheme of things, but from small streams a mighty river can flow.

White and Wrong

As anyone who has been there will tell you, South Africa may well be the world's most beautiful country. Deciding to build Johannesburg where it is, therefore, to make it the biggest city, financial capital and focus of most of the nation's power, is like having a supermodel for a wife and being erotically obsessed with her ingrown toenail.

There are absolutely no compensations to Johannesburg: no beauty, no sights of interest and nothing you couldn't get in any other city, except maybe, a job if you're an African immigrant, a nervous breakdown, shot, stabbed or AIDS. Built on a hot plain on an empty goldmine, Johannesburg looks like LA after the apocalypse, a moon colony abandoned to a thousand years of corruption and disease. Johannesburg is an anti-city, a black hole metropolis where the bleakest predictions of the most pessimistic dystopians have come horribly true. It is, in a word, a shithole and I do not recommend you ever go there.

As horrible as Johannesburg is, it does however fulfil one important function—it challenges you. Not in the conventional *ugly city, bad buses, worse food, murder and mayhem, run for your life* sense that might be true of many destinations; rather it issues a moral challenge. Johannesburg is a looking-glass world where right and wrong are inverted and the moral landscape drops off the map. This city is a vision of life as a merciless Darwinian struggle where the strong are blessed, the meek damned and the demons of race, class, money and violence dance around the funeral pyre, making a mockery of good intentions. Make no mistake, Johannesburg is not a good place. But it can teach you good lessons—most importantly, that almost nothing is certain.

All white South Africans have odd, anachronistic names, as if they were members of a nineteenth-century cricket team or colonial administrators sitting on a porch, drinking gin and complaining about the natives. Clifford was no exception. I had met him the year before while backpacking through Europe. It had been the first major journey of my adult life and our subsequent correspondence was one reason I had decided to make a journey through southern Africa my second.

Clifford lived with his parents in Johannesburg in an expensive suburb in a relatively modest five-bedroom house surrounded by razor wire, steel-reinforced gates and high walls topped with glistening fairy castles of broken glass. As the gate to his driveway slid open on rubber wheels, a white dog the size of a well-fed rabbit appeared, barking madly.

'Our guard dog, Tinkerbell,' said Clifford, his face set in an expression of exaggerated irony. 'My mother's.'

As we pulled into the drive the dog continued its savage attack, little white teeth bared. Getting out of the car,

Clifford quietened her with a few kicks to her fluffy rear and heaved our luggage onto the driveway as the gate closed behind us. A pair of Dobermans suddenly appeared like sinister shadows, weaving between the bags, sniffing at us in a manner that spoke of a casual confidence in their ability to rip our still-beating hearts from our bodies.

Sensing my nervousness, Clifford bent down and ruffled their ears. 'I guess you're looking at all the security,' he said as the dogs padded off. 'I know it seems bad, but we need to be careful. There are so many murders here, and car-jackings all the time.' As he spoke he pointed to bullet holes in the driver's side door of his car. 'They shot four times but only hit twice.' He drilled his finger in up to the second knuckle. 'My mother was driving but she wasn't hurt. A bullet is still in the cavity somewhere. We can hear it rattle when we go round corners.'

As he picked up my bags and took them inside he continued his monologue about life in the world's most dangerous city. 'We haven't had a home invasion. But our neighbour's wife was shot dead three months ago.' He paused a moment before nodding in the direction of their house. 'Nelson Mandela lives in the next block,' he said, as if he were a guide conducting a tour of the stars' homes.

Inside, Clifford's mother greeted us in the kitchen. 'Oh, hello, boys!' she cried; *hello* was *'allo*. 'How are you? I'm Margie. How was your flight? Would you like some popcorn?' She held out an enormous tub, cradled with both arms. 'I'm eating only popcorn during the day this week and drinking banana smoothies at night. People think popcorn is bad for you,' she said, taking a piece between two red fingernails as long as chopsticks. 'But it's actually very low on calories. It's the butter that makes you fat.' Still balancing the morsel in her nails she dropped it into her open mouth, as if being fed by some exotic bird.

Bug-eyed and impossibly thin, Margie cut a startling figure. A flimsy cropped blouse revealed a set of aerobicised abdominals rippling under sun-hammered skin so brown it gave the appearance of having been smoked dry. In both colour and texture her stringy dinosaurian forearms resembled red desert earth, the freckles dotting them the first wet drops of rain. Her dark nimbus of teased hair had the brittle quality of spun sugar; I could have reached out and snapped off a crumbling handful. In high heels and skin-tight jeans belted with ropes of gold chains that matched the chains shackling her neck and wrists, the overall impression was of a bejewelled fondue fork.

'Anything I can do for you boys,' she said, throwing another kernel into her mouth, 'you just let me know.'

Resuming her seat at the kitchen table, Margie set aside her popcorn, picked up the TV remote, extended a red talon and, with studied delicacy, turned up the volume on the set. Satisfied, she picked up a glass of wine and lifted a lit cigarette from the ashtray. 'I'm on a diet,' she announced—*arm awn a die-yit.* 'Wine is okay. But only two glasses and before six o'clock.' The gold bracelets tinkled as she took a slug. 'And never with red meat or root vegetables.'

Just then, a heavy-set black woman in a colourful, shapeless dress appeared. Without acknowledging our presence, she emptied the garbage. An awkward hush fell upon the room. As she shuffled out in a brushed drum of plastic sandals, the bag held before her, Margie turned and addressed us in an exaggerated whisper.

'Our maid, Sunday.' She paused and stared after her, as if watching her through the wall. 'We just caught her stealing.' She shook her head in silent disapproval, a *what-are-you-gonna-do*? look on her face. She took another sip of wine.

'It's terrible,' said Clifford. 'She's been with us for twenty years. When you put that much trust in a person …'

'I know'—*Ah noo*—'she has to support her family in Soweto,' Margie explained. 'But we treat her very well. We pay her far more than many others, so there's no excuse. We won't fire her, but I can't'—*cornt*—'let it go. It's a matter of trust.'

There were a couple of questions I was tempted to ask, questions like how many people Sunday had to support, what being paid 'more than most' meant in Johannesburg, and whether someone working for you for twenty years necessarily made them your friend, especially when they lugged garbage while you sipped wine and did your *White Mischief* routine in the kitchen. Good manners forced me to keep my mouth shut.

'Okay, boys,' said Margie. 'I'm off to yoga now. You have fun.' She drained the last of her wine in one gulp and took off with a pink mat under one arm.

That night I saw my first African sunset. For over an hour we watched as a slab of orange sponge gave way to a rippling blanket of crimson. For a time we stood in silence—Clifford and I—listening to the birdsong and animal noises until the dark came and the curls of razor wire disappeared into the night. It was an awe-inspiring sight and I could see how, despite all the ugliness and danger of Johannesburg, the romance of Africa might find its way into the darkest crevices of this city and, in time, your heart.

With the coming of dark, a new sound joined the cries of dusk as crackling fireworks rippled through the city. What was this, I wondered, a colourful African street carnival or some quaint religious festival?

'Automatic gunfire,' said Clifford, then added reassuringly, 'It's a fair distance away.'

Ah, of course.

Later that evening while exploring the grounds I came across Sunday's quarters, a small extension off the garage. Emanating from inside: harsh fluorescent lights, a blaring television and raucous laughter. Two women—Sunday and another in bright florals—sat in plastic chairs drinking Coca-Cola and slapping their thighs over some private joke.

Seeing me they grew quiet, acknowledging my presence with tight, forced smiles like two prison inmates caught plotting to kill the warden. I nodded my greeting and took off into the dark garden.

I wondered what they did in there at night. I saw them dressing up in stolen clothes and jewellery, doing cruel impersonations of Margie: 'Sunday, I can't find my sunglasses! Sunday, wash my yoga mat! Sunday, oil my hair!'

I had never had anyone wait on me before. It filled me with an overwhelming sense of guilt. This woman was there to do my bidding because some unfathomable quirk of fate had seen me born rich and white, and her poor and black. It shamed me and I vowed she would know it. Sunday would discover I was different to the others. Rather than a distant employer, I would be her friend—a white emissary from a land of freedom and kindness. I pictured myself vacuuming my own room or washing my own dishes while Sunday watched in awe. 'Who is this white boy who cleans his own bathroom?' she would wonder. 'From what strange land does he come?'

Sunday wouldn't know what had hit her. 'Put your feet up, Sunday. Take a break. Never mind me. I'm used to doing all this. Where we come from white people don't have servants.'

'No servants? But how do you clean your homes?'

'Ha ha ha. Oh, Sunday. In my country everyone must do their own cleaning. Everyone is equal there. Although, if you had enough money, you could have a servant yourself.'

'M-m-m-me?' Sunday would stammer. '*I* could have a servant?'

'Yes, Sunday, even you.'

I imagined Sunday after I'd gone, sweeping floors and making beds, daydreaming of this magical place where white people did their own housework. She would be a changed woman. She had seen how life could be. In quiet times she would sit and recall that happy week I had stayed, thinking to herself, 'One day … one day I will leave this life and meet that good boy again.'

In the following days, Clifford showed me around, making a valiant effort to talk up his hometown. 'Look,' he exclaimed as we drove along a ridge overlooking the city. 'The jacarandas are blooming. They're a symbol of Johannesburg.' With their gnarled branches and purple flowers the trees were beautiful. Splashed over the cityscape of Johannesburg, however—with its freeways, brown dome of pollution and the slums on the horizon—they seemed merely part of a bigger ugliness, an algal bloom on the surface of a festering, malevolent lake.

Over the weekend we visited the once-fashionable neighbourhoods of the city, most of which seemed to be in the process of transforming into black ghettoes. In squalid little parks and on street corners, huddles of homeless men stood about clutching plastic bags of solvent, staring red-eyed and menacing. Boarded-up shops dotted the landscape. South Africa's first racially integrated national election had happened only two years earlier and the country was in the middle of what the newspapers described as 'a transition'. In places like Yeoville we walked and ate lunch at kosher restaurants where Israelis with dreadlocks blitzed fruit juices to a trance soundtrack. Clifford called these places 'vibey' and talked up their liberal credentials and racially integrated patrons. Still, it all felt a little on edge, as if everything could go very wrong at any moment.

At a flea market I bought kitschy Nelson Mandela souvenirs and a record called *Sound of the South!*, a 1960s recording by the South African outpost of Up With People, the American 'educational organisation' founded as a clean-cut, commie-free antidote to the hippy movement. The gatefold featured a group of toothy, jug-eared white teenagers in jackets and striped ties strumming guitars and looking like the Mickey Mouse Club if the Nazis had won the war. The songs were a tribute to brotherly love and the dawn of a new era of prosperity in Africa. One number celebrated gold mining, another the African farmer. The liner notes exhorted us to *Switch on, tune in and step out with the fastest-moving people on this continent.*

I looked at the pictures of the kids and wondered where they were now. If they hadn't left South Africa they'd probably be living in a suburban fortress somewhere. Why had they joined the band in the first place? Just to travel and get laid, or had they really believed banging a tambourine would make a difference? Were they as optimistic now as they once had been, or did they look at their country through the bars on their windows and wonder what it had all been for? I saw them in their dark moments retrieving the old instruments from the cupboard, strumming a guitar or blowing on a harmonica and feeling, one more time, the thrill of the past and a time when they were the fastest-moving people on the continent.

The approach of darkness in Johannesburg emptied the streets as the sun withdrew its benevolent influence. At dusk Clifford announced it was time to leave. Dutifully, though not without some resentment, we piled into the Mercedes.

The regimentation of our days in Johannesburg, the constant sense of being corralled and marshalled, was starting to grate. Since arriving I had never experienced a spontaneous moment. From home to car to restaurant to bar to car to home: it was as if Johannesburg was one long, expensively appointed tunnel. Even relaxation was pre-meditated and required props. Everyone here seemed to do yoga, tai chi or stick juggling, all of which just looked like another form of work. You saw them, these white people relaxing, playing hacky sack at the university or power-walking in pristine parks in the better parts of town. You could see the lines of concentration etched on their faces: *I am relaxing now*, they seemed to say; *I am having a good time.* But it didn't look like fun so much as another way of keeping yourself busy, a distraction from the world outside your steel gates and the fact it was falling apart.

As we drove home we spotted a lone jogger speeding past one of the endless concrete walls surrounding the residential neighbourhoods. He was the only white person I was ever to see on the street after 6 p.m. and I applauded his brave defiance of the paranoid conventions of Johannesburg. Of course, he may simply have been running to get home before dark.

———

Clifford was studying economics at university, so the evenings were spent attending parties and *braais* at some of his friends' homes. Almost anywhere else they would have lived in their own apartments or in share houses, but in Johannesburg no one moved out of home until they could afford a fortress of their own.

The security at some homes was arguably more intimidating than the threat of violence it was meant to allay. Most were inside gated communities, forcing everyone to sign in at a guardhouse by the gate, a torch shining in our faces as we awkwardly handed a clipboard around the car. The houses were all the same: vast wastelands of floodlit marble set among groves of lawn tended by blank black faces in denim overalls. All featured standard four-metre walls topped by springs of razor wire, electric fencing, broken glass or combinations of all three. Steel plaques on the gates heralded the protection of various armed response companies: barking dogs in lurid colours; a beefeater standing to attention; a firing machine gun; a charging knight on horseback. My favourite featured a cartoon thief in an eye mask sneaking away with a bag of loot, the jaws of a grinning dog fixed to his backside.

Some of the houses were so huge, their fortifications so complex, they seemed like portals to another time or dimension. Arriving through the automated steel gates put you in mind of the approach to a medieval castle or the inner sanctum of some post-apocalyptic future city where you'd be forced into deadly combat against a motley gang of leather-clad mercenaries and radioactive mutants—*Lifestyles of the Rich and Famous: Beyond Thunderdome*. Windows were cross-braced with giant Xs of steel. Driveways featured spikes embedded in the concrete, ready to be popped up to stop ram raiders. One especially grand home had a dry concrete moat around the perimeter. All had dogs the size of Shetland ponies pacing the grounds. As we said our hellos they glowered menacingly and sniffed at our ankles for the scent of money.

The parties were dire. The men were mostly braying muscle-bound jocks who talked of nothing but rugby, ate with their mouths open and made homophobic jokes. The girls were stuck-up prissy princesses who sat around comparing outfits and complaining of being fat. Whenever they laughed tinkles of gold echoed in the marble rooms.

The racism was, for the most, unexpectedly blatant.

'It's not the blacks you've really got to worry about,' declared one hearty, sausage-chewing throwback. 'It's the coloureds.'

'Yes, apartheid was wrong,' said one girl, 'but the fact is, it was necessary. Without it, we might have been Zambia. Ask the blacks: they were happier before everything became uncertain.'

A discussion about crime—or, more specifically, the supposed white monopoly on being victims of it—forced me to point out that most people murdered in South Africa were black. In response one woman fixed me with an intense gaze and said, 'A black man would never kill another black man.'

In a way it was almost refreshing, this unrepentant prejudice. Before arriving I had imagined the post-apartheid atmosphere to be something along the lines of the German model: don't mention the war unless to apologise profusely. It came as something of a shock, therefore, to discover that not only did a lot of white South Africans seem utterly unremorseful for their nation's recent past, they regarded the era of racial segregation with the same misty-eyed sentimentality as an aged pot head recalling an early Grateful Dead concert. If these were the educated Jewish liberal types, then I dreaded to think what the knuckle-draggers in the sticks were like.

Their lives were oddly contradictory: although they lived with the daily threat of violence, they were totally sheltered and spoiled. They had never done housework, cooked a meal or caught public transport. Their naivety was hilarious. One girl talking of Sea Point, a district in Cape Town known for prostitution, whispered in scandalised tones, 'Well, my friend works for a women's shelter there and she said that most of the customers for the girls are *white* men.' A discussion about South African emigration to Australia prompted one jewel-laden twenty-something to announce, 'I'm not sure Australia is as good as everyone says. I had a friend who moved there, but she said that staff are really *expensive*.'

In South Africa, all your correct, liberal notions of race are turned on their head. Everything you've come to believe about the inherent equality of all people disappears behind these electrified walls. Among these rosy-skinned inheritors of the new nation, the visitor is made to feel as if they were the only sighted man in a land of the blind. *But don't you see?* you wanted to say. *You've got it all wrong!*

But they didn't see, wouldn't, and no amount of reasoning would change their minds. Despite the statistics showing black people were far more likely to be the victims of crime, despite most of these partygoers having no black friends who could either contradict or confirm their assumptions, despite the self-evident logic that wearing gold jewellery and driving brand new BMWs seemed a more probable invitation to crime than a biological predisposition to a lack of melanin, they couldn't help but view the world through the prism of a 1970s blaxploitation film: the brothers were on a mission to get whitey and wouldn't stop until vengeance had been wrought.

Clifford was a little embarrassed by the party. 'I don't really know those guys,' he said as we drove home. 'They're friends of a friend.' But he didn't have to apologise. I said I'd found it interesting, which was true.

At home Margie was in the living room, exercising violently to a video. Tinkerbell ran around her in demented circles, barking. 'Did you have a nice time, boys?' she asked between deep lunges. 'Sunday has made some snacks if you're feeling hungry.'

Laid out in the kitchen were little trays of sandwiches and fried samosas. In my bedroom Sunday had made my bed and was now folding my freshly washed and ironed clothes into a neat pile on the dresser. Immediately I ran over and began to busy myself. 'Oh, don't worry about these, Sunday,' I said. 'I don't need you to do this. Back home, I do everything by myself. Ha ha. I guess we're kind of the same, you and me. Ha ha.' Snatching my clothes from her hands I began manically folding underpants and T-shirts. Sunday just stared at me, confused. 'Oh, yes,' I babbled, 'gotta learn the hard way where I'm from. Cleaning floors, doing the dishes, cooking. The whole lot.' I mimed the actions as I spoke.

Sunday made a few attempts to reclaim her task but I refused. 'No problem,' I said. 'Or "no worries", as we say in Australia. Ha ha ha. We don't have servants there. Nope, everyone's the same in Australia.' I pulled a pair of jeans from her hands. 'Yes, I'll take care of all this. You just go and put your feet up, Sunday. And thanks so much for the sandwiches. I'll enjoy those later. Mm, yummy.' I rubbed my stomach. 'Thanks again, Sunday. Yes, just give me that. You can leave now.'

With a look of utter bewilderment Sunday walked out of the room. I collapsed on my bed clutching a still-warm T-shirt, exhausted by the effort of my own goodness.

After a few days in Johannesburg, the claustrophobia was almost intolerable. Since arriving I had made some tentative excursions outside the marble-and-razor-wire bubble, but never felt that I had been really free. One afternoon, in an especially absurd interlude, I was forced by Clifford to participate in a laser-strike course at the local mall. A notice near the door read: *Please leave all real guns with the attendant.* For the next hour I wandered around a darkened maze, shooting red beams from a plastic gun and making my displeasure plain.

'Shanahan! I shot you,' bellowed Clifford from behind the visor of his futuristic helmet. 'You're dead now. You can't keep walking. You're not taking it seriously!' And I wasn't. Then again, I suppose I could afford not to. For me, running around a darkened room playing shoot-'em-up was for twelve-year-olds' birthday parties and corporate jerks on a company 'bonding' weekend. For people in Johannesburg it was a rehearsal for life.

The world of White South Africa was spirit-crushing. Behind these walls I was a captive, trapped, like the villains from Krypton, in a two-dimensional prison, spinning through space, face pressed to the window, screaming to be let out. As exasperating as the physical limitations were, however, they were only a symptom of the city's deeper, pathological awfulness. Every day I experienced things that made me think Johannesburg had seceded from reality, that inside the bubble we were floating free, unable to tell up from down, right from wrong.

When I baulked at signing a petition against animal testing Clifford was handing about, my objection being that there were people in South Africa living in worse conditions than his Dobermans, he snatched the paper from my hand. 'The poor must help themselves,' he snapped. 'Nobody helps the monkeys!'

At a supermarket I approached a spotty teenager dressed in a trolley-pusher uniform—short-sleeved white shirt, skinny black tie—and asked where the breakfast cereal was. He just shrugged and made an *I dunno* face, so I asked where I could find bread. 'I don't work here!' he snapped, at which point I looked around at the black faces stacking the shelves and realised that, of course, young white people didn't work in menial part-time jobs in South Africa. Why would they, what with the whole *living with their rich parents and not having to* thing, plus the whole *there being plenty of poor black people to do that kind of shitty work* thing, too. In the same supermarket I watched as a bejewelled septuagenarian wearing, I kid you not, a floor-length fur coat, pointed a withered claw at the shelves and barked orders at the ancient black servant pushing her trolley. 'Rice! Oatmeal! Tinned tomatoes! Not those ones, Livingstone. The ones without sugar! How many times do I have to tell you?'

I had to escape, at least for a while. One afternoon, when Margie was at an exercise class and Clifford had gone to visit an ex-girlfriend in hospital, I did just that. With a heavy squeal, the steel gate swung open and I stepped into the leafy deserted street. As I stood looking back at the house, it occurred to me that this was the first time I had been outside the gates on foot.

For some time I walked. First through the suburbs, then along a freeway, my destination little more than a vague notion. In the distance the Hillbrow Tower loomed against the blue sky. It seemed as good a goal as any.

As I climbed the hill, signs of life began to appear. Minibuses loaded with waiting passengers touted for business. Fat ladies spilled from arriving vehicles, coloured turbans on their heads, plastic baskets on their arms. A man pushed a fruit and vegetable cart loaded with an alien's banquet of strange produce. A huge line of schoolgirls in uniform paraded past, hands joined, hair braided in shining plaits, their gazes fixed on me.

In fact, now that I thought about it, everyone was staring at me. It seems idiotic but it took a moment to realise why. As the only white face in a sea of black, I ought to have felt intimidated. But I didn't. Quite the opposite. Being in the street among groups of ordinary people going about their daily business was a thrilling liberation. In contrast to the artificiality and military regulation of life behind the razor wire, the seemingly banal rituals of shopping, lining up at the post office or going home from school took on a festive air, the opening sequence of a musical of which I was the star.

As I walked deeper into the gridded streets of Hillbrow, however, I began to feel apprehensive. A number of apartment buildings seemed to have been taken over by squatters. On street corners, groups of men sat by piles of bedding. Some sniffed glue, others just stood around watching. I powered on, doing my best to appear as though I belonged, as if I was just another local resident out for a stroll. With my head held high and an expression of casual indifference, I tried to ignore the stares.

With every new block the number of men sitting on the footpath grew. As I passed I repressed the urge to look over my shoulder; a signal of nervousness was an invitation to a mugging. Besides, to acknowledge my unease would have been an admission of defeat. My presence here was not only a repudiation of white Johannesburg's paranoia; it was a chance to put my money where my mouth was. After all, wasn't a little part of me secretly very pleased to be the only white man here? *Hi there, folks. How ya doing? It's me, Brendan, just hanging out. Going for a walk. I bet I seem pretty different to a lot of the other white people you've met. But, hey, that's me—I'm crazy! In my eyes, everybody's equal in this big ol' world. Just do good by me and I'll do good by you. That's what I always say.*

The nervous monologue played on a loop in my head as I made my way into the roughest block yet. There were more homeless men here. Pimp-daddy types with dreadlocks, shiny tracksuits and gold chains sat in doorways. Piles of rubbish made obstacle courses on the pavement. A steel rubbish bin issued an acrid tower of smoke. *Don't mind me, folks. Just going for a stroll. My, what a lovely dog you have. I'd probably have that skin condition seen to, though. Yours too. I've never seen a rash that colour.*

Salvation came in the form of a record store. At the door a guard stood clutching a machine gun across his chest. Inside, it was an oasis of calm and order. Rows of CDs and records filled the racks. Promotional material covered the walls. A cardboard cut-out of Mariah Carey welcomed me with open arms.

For a time I browsed the selection. Outside, the light was getting low. The now-familiar dusty gold of Johannesburg was a prelude to darkness. As I clicked through the racks of CDs a large black man approached. 'Excuse me,' he said, his accent testing the boundaries of comprehension. 'Do you have any Namibian music?'

Caught off guard, I looked about the store. 'Ah, I'm not sure,' I said. 'But I saw Nigerian music over that way. Probably near there.' He gave me a surprisingly antagonistic look, as if I were being deliberately difficult, and took off. A few minutes later another approached, his dreadlocks bundled into a Rasta cap like a snood. 'Hey,' he said, unfolding a T-shirt before me. 'Do you have this in extra-large?'

He must have stood like that with the T-shirt unfolded for a full minute before I realised what was happening: because I was white, he, and everyone else, assumed I owned the place. It was a moment of profound revelation. Here I was, still a teenager, wearing torn jeans and a T-shirt that even by the lax hygiene standards of the grunge era was revolting, suddenly catapulted halfway up the social ladder by virtue only of my skin colour.

As someone accustomed to being less than nobody the sensation of automatic power was as thrilling as it was repellent—as if I'd suddenly inherited some titled estate and was now Baron Shanahan of Upper Hillbrow, or something. I saw how you could get used to it. I also saw that race in South Africa was something far beyond the colour of your skin. It was in the air, like a virus— simply to come close was to be infected. The thing that had been created here was beyond human control, a Frankenstein roaming the landscape. We were all potential victims and no amount of good intentions would ever kill it.

I didn't have the opportunity to disappoint him. Outside the store a commotion diverted our attention. Raised voices prompted the security guard to sling his machine gun about threateningly and retreat inside the door. Suddenly, there were a few womanly screams followed by several powerful cracks from a gun. With unhurried but determined strides the man in the Rasta cap made his way to the back of the store. In sharp contrast to his dignified calm, I went to ground, hiding behind the cardboard Mariah Carey.

By the door the yelling continued. Another round of shots was fired, seeming to come from another direction. A hollering chorus rose up punctuated by several more screams, but the action appeared to have moved quickly from the immediate area.

As the excitement died down, the customers in the store gathered by the window and discussed the incident in various languages. The security guard was having a loud conversation with a man on the street. The dark was descending. Police sirens wailed in the distance. I peered through the window and, seeing no dead bodies or any obvious danger, stepped outside.

For a moment I looked around at the streets of Johannesburg. Like the end of a theme park display that begins to right itself for the next showing, things were quickly returning to normal. On the pavements, people had reappeared. Schoolchildren and women walked by unmolested. Homeless men went back to warming themselves over the fire. In the sky, dusty pink stripes were raked against the pale blue. A gorgeous African sunset cast golden triangles on the apartment blocks. A sense of calm reigned. What to do now?

Fuck this, I thought, hustling down the street. *I'm out of here.*

—⁓—

Back at Clifford's home, some of his family had arrived. A cousin and an aunt sat around a bowl of popcorn, chatting with Margie. His elusive father was there, too, back early from the office. Weaving between us, Sunday carried dishes back and forth, setting the table for the evening meal. The atmosphere was convivial and warm and I found myself grateful for the opportunity to relax. Even Tinkerbell was asleep by a low fire. When I told them where I had been they were aghast. I didn't say anything about the shooting.

As I sat down at the kitchen table, Clifford's father peered over the top of a newspaper. 'So, did you see the monkeys in the zoo in Hillbrow?'

Clifford shot him a sharp look, embarrassment written on his face. 'Dad.'

'Well, it's true,' said his father, undeterred. 'That's what they are. With all the bars on the windows and the balconies, they even look like monkeys. A pack of monkeys pissing in their cages.'

At that point Sunday shuffled over clutching a glass of Coca-Cola. She must have heard him but her face registered no reaction.

'You look tired,' she said, smiling and handing me the glass. Desperately thirsty, I drank as she watched and smiled benevolently. I recognised the smile; it was the same she had given me that night when I had seen her in her quarters; the same she had used in the bedroom when I insisted on folding my own laundry. It was the smile of her best behaviour, broad and fake as a three-dollar bill. The smile, I saw now, she used with white people.

Summer Lovin'

Summer in Turkey is the season for women of a certain age. Every year they arrive from all corners of the globe: sharp-faced Finns in blue leather jackets; rotund Germans in hot pants, thighs ringed in pink sunburn; 'free-spirited' Australians draped in ethnic scarves looking to write post-divorce travel memoirs; rough English chain-smokers on package holidays pinching waiters' backsides and having their stomachs pumped; Americans researching goddess worship and looking to have a passionate relationship with someone sensitive to the mysterious tidal rhythms of their yoni.

Turkey is Thailand for women. Unlike Thailand however, where drunk men have sex with poverty-stricken rural teenagers before half-heartedly offering to make them their live-in sex slaves in dungeons in Frankfurt, women who come to Turkey are looking for something more substantial. Love, to be precise. Well, romance at least.

Just as the backgrounds of these women travellers differ, so too do their levels of awareness. A few know exactly what to expect of a local man: he is most likely younger, married, relatively poor, and willing to give her some tooth-rattling sex in exchange for a few free dinners, an iPod and a hollow promise to invest in his cousin's paragliding business. A number, however, are not so wise to reality. Blinded by a longing for romance, they rush headlong into 'relationships' that are doomed to failure, handing over thousands of dollars and vows of eternal fidelity to some carpet dealer or hotel receptionist they met last week at a foam disco, only to rear back in horror six months later when a dumpy woman in a headscarf with three children in tow makes an appearance, demanding to know who this western slut is.

These foreign women form a regiment of the broken-hearted. All across Turkey you meet them: sitting in cafes, reading self-help books; in carpet shops, laughing at the dealer's old jokes; up the back of the tour bus, alone, nose deep in the phrasebook, learning the words for 'I am pregnant'. Of course, not every woman has a bad experience. Some even get married and settle down. These are exceptions. More often there comes a time when the illusion is shattered, when a long-distance romance becomes impractical, cultural gaps become a chasm or, worst of all, the women finally work out they were nothing but a meal ticket in the first place. Whatever the circumstances of their ending, few of these relationships last. Most women go home at the end of the summer. Some stay another season. Others—not many, but a few—never leave. Carol was one of them.

It was October in the southern Turkish resort town of Turgutreis. The yachts in the marina stood empty and covered, their masts clanking soothingly in the breeze. I was there to drop off a package of carpets, a favour for a friend in Istanbul. The dealer collecting them ran a small shop in the tourist part of town. Although the season was over, the water was still warm and the sky clear. I decided to stay a few nights before making my way east along the coast.

Erkan lived in a flat above the shop with Murat, a sixteen-year-old boy to whom he was teaching carpet repair and English. Murat was the son of a distant relative from Cappadocia, central Turkey. The flat was small and Murat slept on the couch in the shop. All day he did the things expected of a Turkish boy in his position: made tea, cleaned the shop, fetched cigarettes and lunch and, in his spare time, sat on the floor, threading a razor-sharp hook through tattered carpets. Brown-legged and beautiful, in the dim light of the shop he was a scruffy angel straight out of a Caravaggio. In a less guarded, more predatory moment I might have described him as jailbait.

'Do you enjoy your life in Turgutreis, Murat?' I asked.

He looked up from his carpet and shrugged. 'Yes, I think is good job.'

'And you don't get bored?'

'No.'

'And you don't feel you work too hard?'

He shook his head and unveiled a crescent-moon smile before returning to his threading, a pretty little angel on the floor, happy with his fate.

For several days the three of us did little but sit in the shop drinking tea, eating meatball sandwiches and smoking hash. In the evening, Murat and I watched pirated DVDs in the flat while Erkan drank and played cards at the yacht club. During the day I sometimes walked about town—doors and windows shuttered for the off-season—or went for a swim in the still-warm water. Mostly, however, I felt no compunction to do anything but surrender to a particularly seductive brand of guilt-free Turkish laziness.

One evening the tinkle of a bell announced the arrival of a visitor. 'Hello, boys,' said Angelique. She unwrapped her scarf and settled into a nest of cushions. 'Look,' she said, holding up a silver block. 'I have brought some *shock-o-lart*.'

Angelique was Belgian and had been living in Turgutreis for two years. She was extremely tall and rail thin with long, straight blonde hair. Now in her mid-forties, Angelique had once run a heavy-metal bar in Belgium, a past echoed in her fondness for black leather pants, Stevie Nicks–style shawls, tasselled leather jackets and quoting Black Sabbath lyrics.

Angelique opened the foil and began to snap off chocolate pieces. 'I have been all day in the hills,' she said, handing chocolate to me and Murat. 'The *shock-o-lart* is good for energy, but not—how do you say?—for the bowels.' She looked around the room. 'Where is Erkan?' she asked.

I told her he had already gone to the club.

'Ah, I see. Well, it is better that he is not here. It means more raki for us!' From the depths of her shawl she produced a bottle of the potent Turkish spirit. Without being asked, Murat got up to fetch some glasses. 'None for you,' said Angelique as he put them on the low table in the middle of the room. 'I know your family would be angry. Good Muslims boys do not drink.' She turned to me. 'I respect the purity of their faith. But it is harsh. It is good for a boy of his age to drink and make sex. To repress the urge is unhealthy. Already in Belgium he would have a wide experience of sexual relations with many women. For this reason prostitution has many social benefits.'

For a while we drank and talked. Angelique was in a buoyant mood. A couple of times she burst into song, complete with air guitar and head banging. 'All day long I think of things but nothing seems to satisfy!' she sang into the silver chocolate bar, a horsetail of hair swishing backwards and forwards. Murat just sat and ate his chocolate, smiling gently.

The ringing of Angelique's phone put the party on hold. She answered it, and an abrupt-sounding conversation in French followed. She sighed. 'Forgive me,' she said. 'It seems my neighbour is in trouble again. I will be back.'

A few minutes later she reappeared with a woman in tow. 'This is Carol,' she announced in the same tone a doctor might say, 'I know it looks awful, but I don't think it's serious.'

Carol was English. She had hair dyed the colour of margarine and was obviously very drunk. Although she was in her late forties, at first I took her to be much older. Bags under her eyes testified to many tired nights; her skin had the unmistakable patina of alcoholism, as if recently scrubbed with steel wool. In keeping with her supposedly carefree life at the beach, her clothes were summery and flowing, her pants tie-dyed. But they were grotty and stained and the soles of her feet, glimpsed through her sandals, were caked with dirt.

'It wasn't my fault,' said Carol to Angelique as she stumbled through the door on ragdoll legs. 'They just don't like me at that place.' She turned and addressed me as if I were an old friend. 'Okay, I admit it,' she said, pressing a hand against her chest to emphasise her sincerity. The pressure made her stagger backwards a little. 'I pissed myself at the bar one time. But it wasn't because I was drunk. I'd been laughing and I have a weak bladder. You think I'm not *embarrassed* about that? You think that's not hard for me to *deal* with?' She turned her attention back to Angelique. 'You know what he's like, Angelique.' It came out *Unsha-leek*. 'He doesn't like me. He hates me, that's all. I'm nothing but an escape goat.'

Carol collapsed by the table and immediately downed the rest of my raki. Angelique sank into the cushions with a look that seemed to suggest she had seen nights like this before. While we drank, Carol continued her furious spiel.

'I don't like that …' She cut herself off mid-sentence and turned to me. 'Everyone knows I don't like the word "cunt". I don't use it, I don't say it and I don't like people who do. Cunt is me-soja-nastic … me-sonja-nest … me-ne-soja-nist … It's not … nice. But I will say cunt this time, because that's what he is: a cunt.' She turned back to Angelique. 'I don't like that cunt. He's only had that bar for a year and he thinks he owns the fucking town. Well he doesn't. And his Irish mate can fuck off back to Belfast if he loves it so much. I told him that tonight.'

To my distress Murat dutifully refilled her glass.

As she downed raki, Carol's anger morphed into depression. She told me about her Turkish ex-boyfriend. She had met him in the nearby town of Bodrum and believed he was going to marry her. So she sold her apartment in London and loaned him almost a hundred thousand dollars. Once he had the money, he took off. Now she was stuck in Turgurtreis, or so she said.

'I loved him! I loved him!' she wailed. 'Oh, Muhammad! Why? *Why?*' She collapsed onto the table and rolled her head in despair.

'It's obvious, Carol,' said Angelique. 'He was an arsehole. He never really loved you and you let him fool you. He was only thirty-four. Everybody told you he was up to no good. Please, stop torturing yourself.'

Carol looked up. Her face wet with tears. 'I still love him! I still love him!' she screamed, almost accusingly. Angelique looked at me as if to say, *This is not going to end soon.*

As Carol's morose ululations continued, the atmosphere grew increasingly awkward. Leaving the subject of Muhammad, she moved on to her brother, who had committed suicide a decade before. Tears streamed down her face as Angelique tried to console her. Attempts to convince her to stop drinking and go home were futile.

After a while, Carol seemed to have worn herself out. Her crying wound down into red-eyed sniffling. Angelique took the opportunity to try to prise the tumbler from her grasp. Suddenly, Carol snatched it back and slammed it on the table. She began to sob into her hands. The tears were different this time, less theatrical. It gave me the uncomfortable sense that something was seriously wrong.

'What is the matter, Carol?' asked Angelique, placing a comforting hand on the other woman's shoulder.

Carol sat up, her face wet with tears. 'I have cancer.'

Angelique's expression was stunned. 'Oh, Carol. I'm so sorry. This is awful.' A host of concerned questions tripped out. What kind? How long had she known? Who had diagnosed it?

'Well,' said Carol, taking another gulp of her raki and staring off into the distance, 'I haven't been diagnosed yet. But I'm pretty certain I have cancer. I'll be dead soon. I'm sure.'

Angelique collapsed back into the cushions. The look on her face was pure fury. Wrapped in her black shawl, she was a huge disgruntled bat. 'Oh my god, Carol. Why do you try so hard to make me hate you?'

'If you don't believe me, then feel the lump!' said Carol, grabbing her bra-less right breast through her shirt. She took Angelique's wrist. 'Feel it!' she commanded.

'I can't feel anything,' said Angelique, dutifully rubbing Carol's breast. 'But I'm not a doctor.'

'I've got cancer, Angelique. Cancer!' Carol's tone became soft and pleading. 'When will it stop? When will the suffering end?'

'Carol,' said Angelique, freeing her hand, 'if you really believe you might have cancer, then you should see a doctor.'

'It's cancer,' sobbed Carol. 'My mother died of cancer and now it's come for me!'

'Your mother died of lung cancer,' said Angelique. 'You need to take control of yourself. You need to stop drinking and calm down.'

With the speed of a striking cobra, Carol snatched my hand. Exhibiting more strength than I would have given her credit for, she plunged it down her top. 'Feel it!' she screamed. 'Feel the cancer!' I did my best to pull my hand away as she rubbed it against her right breast. The skin was soft and papery. The rubbery nipple nuzzled the heel of my hand.

'That is enough!' screamed Angelique, as I pulled my hand free. 'Stop this, Carol.' She grabbed her shoulders and shook her. 'You are hysterical.'

'But what about the cancer!' screamed Carol, reaching into her top and pulling out her breast. All at once, as if suffering a seizure, her body went rigid, eyes clamped shut, her breast mushed between her fingers, the nipple pointed upwards as though aiming at something. Next came a long, high-pitched wail, with an almost operatic gesture. She dropped forward, screaming. As she rolled around among the carpets her breast flopped to and fro like a slowly deflating balloon. 'Oh please, oh please!' she begged. 'Please don't let the cancer take me!'

It was not a dignified spectacle.

Addicts are a quandary. On the one hand, your first instinct is to pity them. They have a disease and are not in control of their behaviour. 'This is the drugs,' you tell yourself as they make their 5 a.m. suicide threat, piss on your carpet or steal the urn with your mother's ashes. But then, sometimes, you find yourself wondering: what if it's not the addiction that's making them behave like arseholes; what if arseholes are attracted to addiction? As much as I know this reasoning to be neither logical nor humane, it can nevertheless be very seductive, especially when the addict's behaviour makes you want to, say, stick their head through a plate-glass window.

In my experience of addiction, alcoholics are probably the worst. Their well of self-pity is bottomless. Carol was a classic case. I felt sorry for her—a bit. There was no doubt she had suffered. Then again, as the received wisdom went, hadn't we all? Everyone's got problems: it's one of those things people say when someone is feeling sorry for themselves. It always seemed silly to me. After all, how is your sister's amputation or the fact your uncle used to feel you up in the bath supposed to make me feel better about my dog dying? Still, it raises an important question: is suffering relative? Can it be charted and graphed, or is it angels on the head of a pin? Is the guy who won't stop crying because his dog died as deserving of our sympathy as the woman in the Sudan whose kids just starved to death?

I once saw an episode of *The Oprah Winfrey Show* about the worst things that ever had happened to people. One guest was a woman with five children. She had gone into a store for five minutes and left them in the car. When she returned the car was engulfed in flames—one of the kids had found a lighter. They all survived but were burned beyond recognition. Some had to wear bandages their whole lives, others had limbs amputated.

I started crying about two minutes into that episode and didn't stop sobbing until well past the end, partly because I was drunk but mostly because it was the saddest story I'd ever heard. Ever since, whenever something bad happens, I think, well, at least all your kids didn't get burned alive in the car, because that seems like pretty much the worst thing that could happen to a person.

But then sometimes I think: hang on, surely there are worse things? What if the same accident had happened to, say, seven kids, or a whole busload? And what if they hadn't survived? Or what if they had, only to die the next year in a plane crash on their Make-A-Wish trip to Disneyland? What about the Holocaust—wasn't that supposed to top the worst-of-the-worst list?

The logical conclusion is that some types of suffering *are* worse than others. After all, surely six million people dying is worse than five kids not dying? So suffering must also be quantifiable. Then again, it might be logically true, but I don't think we really believe it. I doubt if, say, three kids were burned alive in a car anyone would say to their mother, 'Hey, you should see this episode of Oprah. Believe me, it could have been a lot worse.'

So I guess suffering is relative—or maybe it's just about proximity. If the woman from the Sudan was sitting next to me, as opposed to just being a picture on the TV, I'd feel pretty ridiculous crying about my dead dog. Either way, I don't really know. I just try to keep this stuff in mind. It helps whenever some junkie steals my laptop or a drunk starts chewing my ear off about how sad her life is.

⚊⚊

Still sobbing, Carol sat up, her breast hanging out. She turned to Murat with the glazed eyes of the possessed. He, meanwhile, just stared in fascination, as if she were some exotic zoo creature. 'When will it stop?' she said, lifting her breast and thrusting it towards him. 'When's the cancer going to stop?'

Angelique grabbed her by the shoulder and spun her around. 'I'm warning you. Calm down, Carol!'

'But the cancer! The cancer!'

There was a sudden *crack*. It took a moment to register what had happened—until then I had never seen a woman slapped who wasn't in black-and-white and standing opposite Clark Gable. I ought to have been shocked. And I was, momentarily. The truth is, however, that it was exciting more than anything.

Slowly Carol turned back, her mouth open. She began to make a low whining—the first moments of an air-raid siren. Angelique grabbed her firmly by the shoulders. 'Now calm down,' she said, a scolding finger pointed into Carol's face.

'I'll die before the cancer takes me,' whimpered Carol. 'I'll kill myself!' Her neck went slack and her head began to roll. Angelique grabbed her by the chin. Her fingers were dug deep into Carol's cheeks, squeezing her mouth open into a figure eight.

'The problem is not cancer, Carol,' said Angelique. 'The problem is your drinking. I have told you before. You need to stop drinking. Everyone is sick of it. It's not just bad for you. It's bad for your family, your friends and everybody who knows you.'

'But the cancer,' said Carol, her lips moving like a feeding fish's.

Angelique screamed in frustration. I supressed the instinct to yell, 'Hit her again!'

Angelique let go. 'Enough!' she said as Carol rolled around on the floor, moaning as if in pain. 'Murat, go and see if you can find someone who can drive her home. This is the last time.'

Why are we so attracted to the notion of love in foreign places? Why do we romanticise and exoticise people who speak with a different accent, pray to a different god or watch *Who Wants to Be a Millionaire?* in a different currency? Is it the people themselves we imagine to be better, or does the very fact of being somewhere unfamiliar allow us to hope that, for some reason, this time it will be different?

Arriving in a new country it can sometimes feel as if anything is possible. This is not unreasonable. After all, you just flew through 10 000 kilometres of clouds in a tin can. Routine dulls our sense of wonder; travel reawakens it like water poured on a wilting plant. At home we have long stopped noticing the little details. In a new country we acquire super-senses. Everything is interesting: the smell of the air, the combinations on the licence plates, the way people hold their cigarettes or stack fruit in the grocery stores. If people seem more attractive, it's probably only because we're looking more closely.

Our sense of wonder and excitement in the face of newness can, however, have an unintended consequence. We turn our experience into a spectacle; we become viewers rather than participants. Sometimes it feels that the streetscapes are sets and the people actors going about their daily lives for our benefit. It's tempting, therefore, to cast ourselves in a role: the noble loner roaming the world in search of enlightenment; the fancy-free vagabond who laughs in the face of danger and tweaks the nose of death; the passionate exotic beauty who has been hurt by love but who, under a gentle hand, will learn to feel again.

This play-acting is liberating and fun—it gives us a chance to be the centre of attention, to retell our best jokes and puke in the street where nobody knows us. But it is also a lie. Life doesn't get better just because we change the scenery. Travel distracts us from the nagging doubts, the shame and regret—it ensures we'll never bump into our ex at a bar or have to drive past the school where we were bullied—but the past is a ball and chain we can only ever hope to accommodate, never free ourselves from. When we travel we might lose our bags, but we'll never lose our baggage.

The next night Murat, Erkan and I all went to Angelique's house. She greeted us at the door with a smile, a kiss and a glass of wine. 'I'm so happy you could come,' she said. Warmth and friendliness radiated from her, drawing us in. As she wrapped her arms around me I felt the soft brush of the tassels on her leather jacket and inhaled the scent of expensive upholstery.

While Angelique cooked, we drank wine and listened to obscure heavy metal. The previous night had ended much the same way. Murat had eventually found a taxi willing to take Carol. The four of us piled in, Carol sobbing in the front seat. When we reached her house, Murat walked her inside. Then we went next door to Angelique's house and drank wine while discussing the events of the evening. Murat said Carol had refused to go to bed so, after an hour, we sent him over to check on her. He came back a little while later to report she was asleep on the couch. After another hour or so at Angelique's, Murat and I went back to the shop.

Angelique sighed and stirred her pasta. 'I like Carol,' she said. 'When she's sober, she's fine. The problem is, these days, she's almost never sober. If she doesn't stop drinking soon, I don't think I can help her for much longer. Unfortunately this is what happens to alcoholics—one day they wake up and realise no one is there to take care of them anymore. Look what happened to Ozzy Osbourne when the band replaced him with Ronnie James Dio, you know?'

Erkan asked whether she had heard from Carol since last night.

Angelique laughed wearily. 'She came over here this afternoon. She was drunk again, of course. She started to abuse me. Can you believe it? She said I had left her door unlocked all night. That anyone could have got in.' Angelique shook her head. 'She screamed at me and said I was a bad friend and accused me of letting rubbish blow on her property. Then she got really crazy and—get this!—accused *him* of trying to rape her!' She pointed to Murat. He was sitting across the room, smiling shyly as he nursed a Coke. 'I mean, come on!'

We laughed. The suggestion was absurd: why would this gorgeous teenager be interested in a scrawny old soak like Carol? Erkan, clearly disgusted by the accusation levelled at his cousin, said, 'Turkish boys are desperate, but not that desperate.'

We laughed again, louder this time—except Murat, who was absentmindedly running a finger around the rim of his glass. I looked at him and he met my eye with a smile. But it was a different smile. Not the smile of a shy angel in a painting but devilish and sly. A smug smile. A smile of complicity. A smile that said he knew he had got away with it.

Oh, he had done it alright. The little shit.

As the music played and the conversation turned to other things, I thought of Carol. I could see her now: sitting on the couch sobbing, mourning love's broken promises, wondering how it had all gone wrong, why she hadn't written herself a better script. Did she really believe she had cancer? Did she secretly hope for it? Perhaps she would have liked to end it like her brother but lacked his will. I guess you could say she was just feeling sorry for herself. But, then again, that's what people do. And why not? After all, sometimes there's nobody else to do it for us.

Filler in Manila

Since I was old enough to eat solid food my teeth have been the bane of my existence. As a child the exit of every baby tooth signalled not the excitement of money under the pillow but the growth of some new tortured shard from the cave roof of my mouth. At night I would lie awake, plagued by images of archaeologists retrieving my skull from ancient strata, taking one look at my jaw and returning to the drawing board to add a new branch to the tree of human evolution.

By the time I reached high school my teeth looked like a hillbilly's garden fence, an impression only enhanced by a vicious beating in my late teens that left me with several large chips and a blackened shingle where my right front tooth should be. Around the time I turned thirty the seismic gyrations of my wisdom teeth were creating hideous infections, shoddy stop-gap dental work from childhood was crumbling and my right incisor became horribly twisted, clamping my tongue at unexpected intervals. Without the money required to fix these problems, it seemed I had two options: a pair of pliers and a future of blended foods, or getting my teeth fixed in a country where people live in cardboard boxes by the rail-way track.

⟶

Telling people you are taking a dental holiday to the Philippines elicits various reactions, ranging from well-intentioned warnings about the standard of hygiene in developing countries to earnest enquiries as to whether your new teeth are the first stage on your journey to becoming a woman. Many countries now offer so-called dental tourism, so my choice of the Philippines was to some degree arbitrary. If pressed, however, I would say I chose it partly because I had a friend living in Manila, partly because Filipino dentists have a good reputation, but mostly because, of all countries, perhaps none better understands the importance of glamour.

Filipinos love glamour. In fact it's probably fair to say it's the closest thing they have to a national ethos: glamour is to Filipinos what discipline is to the Japanese, *joie de vivre* to the French and hating success to the English. This unique emphasis on glamour means that Filipinos have a high tolerance of personal vanity—looking good is not a choice, it's a public duty.

From a young age Filipinas are encouraged to enter beauty pageants or talent contests. Wearing full make-up and marvellous crinoline dresses trimmed with sea froths of lace, they float onto stages singing karaoke versions of the songs of Barbra Streisand, Celine Dion or any other act that could conceivably be impersonated by a drag queen.

Being glamorous is enough to earn you forgiveness for almost anything in the Philippines. For decades Imelda Marcos bled the country dry, but she now lives in suburban Manila, unmolested and idolised simply because the nation admires her outfits. 'It is against religiosity to be surrounded by ugliness,' she once said. In the Phillippines, glamour is not merely a public duty but a sacred obligation.

This attitude is a refreshing inversion of the commonly held notion that looking good is the preoccupation only of superficial dimwits. As a writer I'm supposed to be monkishly indifferent to my appearance. Wrinkles, glasses, ear hair: these are to be not merely tolerated but celebrated, physical proof of my disdain for the crass artifice of the physical world. The writer who indulges in personal vanity is liable to set themselves up for a very public shaming. When English novelist Martin Amis had his teeth reconstructed he was the subject of widespread ridicule in the British press, his need for a functioning mouth gleefully set upon as evidence of his long-suspected shallowness. Mr Amis has my sympathy. My writing may never reach his giddy heights but my teeth … well, my teeth are Nobel Prize material.

A week after booking my ticket I arrive in Manila knowing nothing about the place. My first impression is that it is rougher than I'd expected. While neater and cleaner than some Asian capitals, the poverty seems harsher and more desperate. At the airport I fight my way through a football riot of returning maids and hail a taxi. As we move off a tiny beggar child approaches me. I check my pockets but have nothing to give, no coins, not even a pencil or a sweet. Not easily deterred, he grabs the door as I try to close it and is almost sucked under the wheel as we speed away.

I soon realise my taxi driver has no idea where he is going. His technique is to simply announce the name of every new street as we turn into it. It is annoying but gives me time to think, and to examine the city by night. As we make our way slowly through the streets it occurs to me that I know nothing about my dentist, Dr Filomena. I have a recommendation via a friend of a friend, but is that good enough? How competent is he? What schools did he attend? What if he knocks me out and I wake up with my pants around my ankles in a room full of people wearing Venetian masks?

As I gaze out the window to a soundtrack of the driver's chants—Salcedo, Rufino, Legazpi—I notice that dental surgeries seem to be on every corner. Some look less like medical facilities than refreshment stands or illegal cock-fighting venues. One—all lit in glamorous neon, as if it were a very small, very shabby casino—is called the Pray To God Dentist. Unfortunately, one of the letters is malfunctioning so it reads 'Pray To Go'. I am suddenly struck by a fear that my snap decision to have dentistry in the Philippines is a dangerous folly.

The next morning I arrive at a skyscraper in Makati City, Manila's surprisingly orderly business district. Outside the elevator leading to my dentist's office is a large, badly painted picture of the Virgin Mary under the caption *Please*

Pray the Rosary. This does little to assuage my fears. I have no particular objection to public religion, but prayer is not something you necessarily want to rely on at the dentist, the godless terrestrial comforts of a good-sized injection of codeine being infinitely preferable to the nebulous assurances of the Catholic doctrine of intercession. Besides, what happens if I don't floss? Fifty Hail Marys?

At the office I fill out forms and peer into the surgery. Aside from the large crucifix on the door it seems like any other I've ever seen. My dentist, however, is not. Vivacious in a uniquely Filipino way, Dr Filomena is a ball of energy—literally. Four feet tall and massively overweight, she looks exactly like a ball.

'Just call me Dr Fifi,' she says. 'Everybody does!'

Dr Fifi? This will not do. Fifi is a name for poodles and strippers. I want my dentist to have a solid, dependable name like Dave, Chuck or Abe. I want my dentist to have the reassuring, unflappable temperament of a war hero and the freshly scrubbed waspishness of a Mormon pastor. Discovering your dentist is called Dr Fifi is like strapping yourself into an aeroplane and hearing, 'This is your captain, Sparkle, speaking.'

With great trepidation, I take my place in the chair.

As Dr Fifi begins her examination my anxieties are quickly dispelled. Her respectful explorations of my mouth and her seemingly genuine concern for my welfare are in sharp contrast to the indifferent simian grapplings I have endured in dental chairs at home. After a while, my only reservation is her fondness for 1970s soft-rock classics, karaoke videos of which she plays endlessly on a DVD player six inches from my face, as if using some diabolical cultish hypnosis technique.

With a mouth full of rubber fingers I explain I want two porcelain crowns and whatever else she think I need in the time I have.

'How long are you in the country?' she asks.

'Five days.'

'Oh dear God!' says Dr Fifi, with typical Filipino candour. 'These teeth are more like five months. But we'll see what we can do.'

To the tune of Air Supply's 'I Want to Know What Love Is', we get down to business.

There are a few things about the Philippines I notice immediately. One is that every second woman is pregnant. This is why there are ultrasound and neonatal clinics everywhere, some with wacky names like Womb with a View, Womb to Move and Womb and Board. Filipinos, I am to discover, have a zany sense of humour.

So many women are pregnant because Filipinos are very religious. Trucks drive around covered in airbrushed images of Jesus and there are special parking spots for priests. In a shopping mall one afternoon I walk out of Zara to discover a full-scale church service being conducted in the walkway, complete with a priest in robes and tiny altar boys shaking incense burners. At first I don't know what to do—it seems disrespectful and weird to keep shopping in front of all these praying people. But in the end I just follow everybody else and walk around the kneeling worshippers to the Levi's store.

Like most of Asia, the Philippines has a fascination with skin-whitening cream. You can even get a product specifically for the vagina and anus. One of the regular varieties I see advertised comes in two types: 'classic white' or 'pinkish white'. Walking the streets I often see women who obviously use skin lighteners on their faces. They're easy to spot because the result is strange: it doesn't make them look white so much as grey, like a faded black-and-white photo.

Perhaps an extension of their mania for beauty products is the Filipino obsession with 'feminine hygiene'. Ads for vaginal douches are everywhere. The number of competing brands is incredible, as is the variety of scents they offer—everything from 'Blossom' to 'Light Floral' to 'Morning Paradise'. In the Philippines your vagina could have a fragrance for every season. Winter is pine with a touch of leather. Spring is jasmine blossom. Summer brings notes of ripe tropical fruit. Autumn offers the comforting warmth of cinnamon with a base note of apple pie and just a hint of wood smoke. In a department store I imagine a testing counter staffed by female assistants: hitching their skirts, they dip little strips of cardboard then wave them under the noses of browsing shoppers.

One of my favourite of these products is called Gyne-Clean. The TV commercials feature a woman in flowing linen stretched out on a couch, saying, 'I'm not just clean; I'm Gyne-Clean.' The friend I am staying with and I are obsessed with this ad. I spend a lot of time lying on the couch, spreading my legs, bending forward to inhale deeply then saying, 'I'm not just clean; I'm Gyne-Clean.'

Before I leave, as a present for letting me stay, I buy my friend a jumbo-sized bottle of Gyne-Clean and, for her husband, a soap for washing your foreskin called Peni Fresh. It boasts of having a 'delicious tutti-frutti flavor'. When I leave I write a thankyou note and make sure to put the gifts somewhere the maid will see.

Perhaps the strangest thing about Filipinos is their names. Having a dentist called Dr Fifi is, by Filipino standards, pretty unremarkable. In fact, it's probably safe to say that Filipinos have, hands down, the stupidest names in the world. This is a country where grown men are called things like Babe or Pingpong. Where parents call their children DongSquared or Ding2 to make DongDong or DingDing sound classier. In the Philippines there is no need for a showbiz pseudonym when the TV stars have real names like Pepsi Paloma and Pops Fernandez.

Unlike in the west, crazy made-up names are not the sole domain of the *Jerry Springer* classes. A congressman, for instance, is called Ace Barbers and the president has two sisters: Pinky and Ballsy. Doorbell names, so-called because they sound like a door chime, are everywhere. When one politician was asked why his name was Bing he replied, with no trace of irony, 'Because my brother's name is Bong.'

Hybrids, in which parents combine their names, are also popular. My friend swears she knows a couple called Arsenio and Maria who christened their daughter Arsemarie. Outright jokes, too, are not unheard of. Identical twin girls who live in the building where I'm staying are called Kate and Replikate. It makes every LaFonda and Quintavarius on *The Ricki Lake Show* bickering over whether they should call their kid Cupcake or D*Shawn look like model parents.

***

For the next few days my world is a marathon of drilling, sawing, scraping and the greatest hits of Boston. Stuck in the chair with my vision restricted to the range of my rolling eyeballs gives me a lot of time to get to know Dr Fifi's ceiling. For five days I am an explorer on a tiny continent, examining every square inch from the window to the waiting room.

Other than a faded Philippine Airlines sticker inexplicably pasted in one corner, there is little of interest. My attention soon turns instead to the hygienist. She is young and very tiny, her face utterly impassive. She wears a name tag that says *Rosemarie*, but gives nothing else away. Sometimes Dr Fifi is a bit of a bitch to her. She never speaks to Rosemarie in English, only Tagalog, and only then to reprimand her or tell her to fetch something. All day she hands tools to Dr Fifi with the same look of resigned indifference. I think she's bored, or maybe the karaoke videos have done their job and turned her into a compliant robotic slave.

The more I examine Rosemarie's face, the more I realise she and Dr Fifi look alike. Despite the fact one is considerably fatter than the other, their eyes and mouths are almost identical. I wonder about their relationship. Is it merely professional or is she some country cousin come to the city, given a job out of charity? She probably doesn't get paid much. I imagine Dr Fifi's passive-aggressive reminders of her benevolence; how Rosemarie would be back in the rice paddy if it wasn't for her. Then I see Rosemarie suddenly cracking one day, picking up a probe and sticking it in Dr Fifi's eye, blood spraying across my face and into my gaping mouth.

This is how I pass the hours.

Not all of my time is spent at the dentist. The evenings give me a chance to explore Manila. Like my teeth, it's not pretty but it has character.

Everyone here is always putting on a show. It doesn't matter what you look like or your level of ability, in Manila you are always expected to be 'on'. With so many people looking to make it—new ones born every day—competition in entertainment is high. In this town when someone asks 'Whaddya got?' you'd better be ready to wow them, otherwise your audience will just head down the street to see the guy who juggles babies or the woman whose vagina smells like a fresh-baked chocolate cake.

Deformity is no barrier to being a performer in the Philippines. In fact, it's an asset. There's a bar here called Hobbit House that is completely staffed by little people who regularly perform a song-and-dance routine, shaking pompoms while wearing T-shirts that read I ♥ Midgets. You could argue this is exploitative, but in a country where everyone is being exploited—whether it's making clothes or working at a call centre—no one seems to really mind, least of all the little people. Later that night, on the other side of town, I discover you can actually go and see a midget oil-wrestling competition. Deformity, I conclude, is just another niche in the Philippines, a way to stand out from the crowd. In a country where everyone's a star, it's preferable to being forgettable.

That night, as if to confirm my thesis, we are drinking on the street when a transvestite with one eye sidles up and starts a sexy bellydance routine for change. Her face is pancaked in lead-white makeup; you can see into the hollow of her eye socket and flashes of her well-stocked jock regularly appear from under her skirt. In any other context she would have been nightmarish. In Manila she's just another girl looking for her big break.

Even the news is entertaining in the Philippines. The anchors use hilarious outdated slang and make bitchy asides about starlets who have gained weight. While I am in Manila a man is murdered and his girlfriend badly bashed in their apartment in what the papers described as a 'posh' part of town. In an apparent attempt to pin the killing on the victim's stepbrother—a powerful, fabulously wealthy businessman—his name is written in blood on the wall.

The murder sparks a war between two rival Manila families and I find myself becoming obsessed with the case. Once I return home I follow it online. When it is discovered that the stepbrother has an alibi and that suspicion has shifted to the girlfriend, I can't say I am really surprised. But still: a name in blood on the wall. That is a nice touch. Even murder in the Philippines has a sparkle of Old Hollywood.

On the fourth morning I casually mention to Dr Fifi that a six-month-old filling is hurting. After an X-ray and a bit of exploratory drilling, she announces I need a root canal. Deciding I might as well get it done while I am here, I settle down to a seven-hour marathon of Doobie Brothers and drilling.

Unfortunately it is soon established that I have 'hidden roots' not visible on the X-ray. This is a bummer for two reasons: there may not be enough time to finish before I leave, and the only way to find them is to poke until I scream. I am too tense to explore the landscape of the ceiling anymore. The pain makes me forget the sticker and the hygienist. Hail Marys are all I have now.

On my final night I walk with my friend to the red-light district for a farewell drink. Though tempted by the spectacle of foxy boxing we soon find ourselves at the centre of an impromptu beauty pageant. So graceful and glamorous are the girls marching down the street, each on the arm of a well-starched suitor, it takes us a while to realise that most are prostitutes from the surrounding brothels. A number of those are transvestites.

Thrilled by this spectacle of authentic Filipino glamour I approach to take photos. One elegant transvestite twirls her snow-white hoop skirt for me then immediately tries to extort money. When I refuse her eyes narrow and, for a moment, I think she might be about to pull a knife.

'You want to be in the parade?' she asks, fluttering her false eyelashes. 'I think you are very handsome.

The next day, my last with Dr Fifi, is a race against the clock. She starts with the attachment of my new porcelain teeth. They make me look so good I forget all about my hangover, the pain and the fact that by day's end I will have heard the theme to *Greatest American Hero* more than ten times.

In the mirror I gnash and grind my teeth like a speed addict. They're still far from perfect but the improvement is remarkable. I think of all the years of self-consciousness I have endured. I remember every family snapshot and school yearbook: photographers kneel before me, begging for a smile, only to rear back and cover their eyes in terror, disavowing the existence of God. I picture with resentment the face of the cheap Irish dentist my parents used to take me to. An Irish dentist—it was just rubbing salt in the wounds. Like forcing a child with a growth disorder to see a Kalahari Bushman.

As I look at my teeth I see a three-dimensional portrait of all my neuroses, doubts and failings. They are, I realise, stand-ins for everything I don't like about myself—each canine a memorial to defeat, every incisor the keystone of my anxiety. I hate them, but they have been with me every day. They are a part of me. Am I so prepared to jettison this part of my body that has mapped my life, the tree rings of my seasons?

Too late for all that now.

I lie back in the chair. Air Supply is playing. A woman on the video steps across a Chinese bridge and fiddles with some spring blossoms. I look at Rosemarie, staring at the back of Dr Fifi's head. Is it resignation or psychotic anger in her eyes? I decide to do something I should have done a long time ago. Taking the spit tube from my mouth I sit up. 'Please, Dr Fifi,' I say. 'Would you turn the music off?'

In DC Proposal

The Norwegian had been trouble from the start. I had sensed it the moment he sat down next to me in the TV room and proudly produced his Jackie Kennedy commemorative teaspoon.

'I went to the John F. Kennedy Library today,' he announced in that strange accent all Scandinavians seem to have, like a backward-playing record. 'I bought this.' From within a crumpled paper bag he produced the silver spoon, a profile of the former First Lady at its tip. 'You see it is beautiful.' He mimed stirring a cup of tea inches from my face, smiling gently as if I were mentally disabled or he was trying to hypnotise me. 'Now when I am drink tea I will think of her. Oh, Jackie,' he said, his tone becoming wistful. 'It was a sad life. But she was always so prit-ee.' With that, he carefully rewrapped the spoon and forced the package back into the bulging green nylon bag strapped about his waist that he referred to as his 'funny pack'.

It was the day before New Year's Eve in Washington DC, the third day of the blizzard, the worst in living memory. On the streets the snow was chest-high. Through frozen white walls pedestrians shuffled, heads bowed like shameful geishas. On the roads there was traffic chaos; cars launched onto pavements, upending garbage cans, skiing past star-tled pedestrians and bowing lampposts like drinking straws. Getting out of the city was next to impossible. Trains and buses were booked solid and the highways looked as if there'd just been an announcement of an alien invasion. I had been in Washington five days and, it seemed, would be here a few more.

'Soon I will go to New York,' said the Norwegian, fiddling with the zipper on his funny pack. 'There I will see the Museum of Modern Art and maybe go skating at the Rockefeller Centre. Oh, it will be so beautiful. Just like *Breakfast at Tee-fanny's*.'

The Norwegian was in his late forties, which, as anyone who has spent any time in youth hostels can tell you, is a bad sign—any man old enough to be earning real money doesn't want to share a dorm room with a group of unwashed teenagers unless he is homeless, pathologically cheap or has a dirty-underpants fetish. Odds were, this guy ticked at least two boxes. Nevertheless, as anyone who has stayed in youth hostels can also tell you, there is almost no other environment in which you learn so quickly to lower your standards.

From food to bed linen to personal hygiene: through the looking-glass of communal living, real-world rules fray and crumble, and nothing goes quite so quickly as the standard of company you keep. Starved for friendship and conver-sation, solo travellers soon find themselves drawing from some very dry wells: stony-faced Germans with louse-ridden dreadlocks; surly, tight-fisted Israelis in tie-dyed parachute pants; a million dreary Cindys and Mindys with etherised grins and a comprehensive knowledge of the best public toilets in Europe. In youth hostels, people you'd normally have nothing to do with are suddenly elevated to the status of your new best friend, called upon to act as the rent-a-crowd for your depressing birthday party or to share the costs of renting a car, only to disappear as quickly as they arrived, your relationship memorialised by the cameo in the fading snapshot by the Eiffel Tower, an email address written on a crumpled napkin or the knowledge that there's always a bed waiting should you ever be unfortunate enough to step off a bus in Boise, Idaho, at 3 a.m.

The White House Hostel was no exception. In addition, however, to the usual assortment of dreary Scandinavians and belligerent Irishmen there were also an unusually large cast of oddballs, exceptional in their strangeness even by the standards of transient living.

In a room next to mine was a middle-aged alcoholic who, according to the complaints of the Swiss girl sleeping on the bunk above him, peed into a Coke bottle rather than using the toilet at night. This behaviour was a source of understandable disgust to the man's roommates, especially the deranged hobo in the corner who had a toy trailer by his bed stacked with a two-foot-high pile of Bibles that he obsessively annotated with messages to God and images of demons and decapitated women. In the afternoons he could be found sitting in the common room, drinking instant coffee, thumbing his Bibles and muttering to himself like an unattended ham radio.

My room was not without its share of characters. Occupying a bunk opposite my own was a man who did little more all day than sit and stare into the distance, consuming packets of Cheetos with the stoic determination of a Galapagos tortoise. Although not much older than myself, his physical appearance was alarming: his hair white-blond and his face puffy and red, as if he had been stung by a bee and was going into anaphylactic shock. Around his mouth a constant halo of luminous orange gave him the appearance of being midway through the application of clown make-up. For reasons unclear, he sometimes wore a neck brace. The Galapagos tortoise rarely spoke. Occasionally, however, he would take a break from his constant eating and buttonhole some unfortunate passer-by, regaling them with monologues on apparently innocuous topics—the snow, say, and its role in the international Jewish banking conspiracy.

Making even these crazed drifters seem mildly eccentric by comparison was a middle-aged Japanese woman, clearly in the grip of some sort of mental collapse, who first came to my attention in spectacular style moments after my arrival at the hostel. While I was still signing the register, she marched into the common room and tipped a basket of laundry on the floor. After a brief pregnant pause she unleashed a series of vicious Oriental curses and began flinging an assortment of soiled underpants and bras at her unfortunate bunkmate, forcing her to shelter behind a couch. Eventually she was restrained by some of the other guests and marched back up to her room. An hour later she could still be heard shrieking and cackling to herself like a mad aunt in the attic.

Among this deranged menagerie it was difficult to imagine that anything short of, say, an attached foetal twin could mark you as exceptionally peculiar. But there was one inhabitant of the White House Hostel who made me even more uncomfortable than all the others combined.

Edward was a black albino from New Jersey and my friend by attrition. Wherever I went, he seemed to be: in the subway station lurking behind a pillar, in the Cezanne room at the art gallery, or, as on one memorable occasion, appearing as if in an elaborate magic trick from behind the marble throne of Abraham Lincoln. No matter what precautions I took, Edward was impossible to avoid. After a while, these accidental meetings became so frequent I began to wonder whether he might not be actively stalking me. On the face of it the idea seemed ridiculous—such coincidences happened often while travelling. Still, I couldn't help but feel there was something disturbingly obsessional in Edward's persistent campaign to befriend me.

It wasn't that Edward was objectionable. In fact, in some ways, he made a good companion. He was mild-mannered and polite to a fault, his conversation banal. He rarely spoke without being asked a question and the information he offered revealed little more than the sketchy details of a lifetime spent living with his parents and playing *Dungeons and Dragons*. Physically he presented no threat: his build was slight, his voice soft and reedy. Like a lot of albinos he had eye problems and wore thick glasses. Altogether, he presented an apparently benign figure, so it seems ridiculous to admit that I found him unnerving to the point of being sinister.

Edward's passivity disturbed me. There was something ominous in his silence, as if he were an alien sent to earth to study human behaviour and I his subject, in danger at any moment of being spirited away and vigorously probed before being pickled in formaldehyde. This impression was only heightened by his unusual physical appearance. While I had seen albino black people before, I had never been on close terms with one and am forced to admit I found his features both repellent and fascinating in equal measure. His skin was white to the point of transparency, except for his broad nose and thick lips that were splattered with coffee-coloured patches like cruel beauty spots. His hair was short and slightly golden, a swim cap of afro curls about his scalp. His hands were bright pink, as if they'd been dipped in scalding water. When he frowned, crimson creases bloomed on his forehead. Contrary to what I had been taught, Edward's eyes were not pink but a kind of dull grey; behind his glasses they loomed huge and googly, like some strange, exotic fish staring back at me through the glass of an aquarium.

Sharing a room made attempts to avoid Edward especially difficult. Apparently innocuous conversations about my plans for the day became torturous webs of deceit as my efforts to exclude him from my sightseeing expeditions grew increasingly elaborate. I took to making mental notes of places he had already been in order to discourage him.

'Where are you going this morning?' he asked me one day.

'Ah … I'm off to the Air and Space Museum,' I said, recalling an excruciating conversation two days earlier about the difficulties of eating chips in zero gravity.

'I've already seen it,' he said despondently.

'Oh well, that's too bad.'

'It's okay,' he said wearily. 'I can go again.'

My efforts to avoid Edward were complicated by a two-fold guilt. First, I felt ashamed that I should not want to be the friend of someone who so badly wanted to be mine. Second, I was paranoid he might think I was snubbing him because of his condition.

I am aware of the hypocrisy inherent in my fear of offending Edward. After all, if I honestly didn't care what he looked like and truly regarded him as an equal I would have stopped patronising him and simply told him to leave me alone. A misguided sense of charity, however, wouldn't allow it. Edward's almost parasitic neediness betrayed, I felt, a personality scarred by a lifetime of rejection. It had occurred to me that our friendship—if you could call it that—was probably the latest in a long line of such fleeting encounters and I didn't want to add to what must have been an already rich store of humiliation. As if I were dealing with an abused puppy that kept pissing on the carpet, I could react only with patience. Chained to Edward by the bonds of guilt and social awkwardness, I resolved to endure his presence until either one of us left, or fate intervened.

'At home I am a feesh-er-man,' said the Norwegian, reclining into the velvet sofa. 'I have a boat. We catch many types of fishes but I don't know the names. In Norwegian some are called by the names of the Russians. Other fishes we call by ourselves. Some we use in English.' He laughed softly and readjusted his funny pack. 'But then sometimes we have fights with the Danish people. They have also names for fish. But crazy names! Danish people have crazy fish.' He laughed again, harder.

For the last twenty minutes I had endured a number of similar monologues. Topics ranged from his desire to see Siegfried and Roy in Las Vegas to the difficulty of obtaining a certain kind of herring in American supermarkets. All of it was conducted in a fractured, albeit not entirely charmless, English, peppered with curious turns of phrase that had obviously been through several mistranslations. On one occasion he announced that, 'People who live under glass houses no stones must throw.' On another he expressed a desire to 'go where I will be blown by the wind'. It was almost worth hanging around for.

Taking a pause in the conversation about North Sea fish stocks as my cue, I stood up and announced my retirement.

'Well, I'm off,' I said, stretching and trying to look as weary as possible.

'Oh, you are slippy?'

'Excuse me?'

'Slippy … *slippy*. You want to go in the slip.'

'Yes,' I said cautiously. 'I think so.'

Upstairs, the dorm was empty but little mementoes of the other residents remained. A dusting of Dorito crumbs, a gift from the Galapagos tortoise, covered my blanket. A reeking wet chamois had been laid to dry on the cross bar of my bedpost. In a corner of the room a bag of garbage, untouched since my arrival, had been opened by what could only have been a rat.

After shaking off my blanket and knocking the chamois to the ground, I settled into bed. For a while I made no effort to sleep, just watched the snow fall outside the barred window, the fluffy balls illuminated by the streetlight, and wondered when I might leave. It wasn't that I resented being stuck in Washington. In fact, in spite of the snow, I liked it.

There is a tendency, even subconscious, to think you know Washington; it is, after all, possibly the most personified city in the world. People from Uruguay to Uzbekistan are constantly hearing about what 'Washington thinks', the trade deals 'Washington is moving to secure', the conspiracies 'Washington is concocting'. To most people,

Washington might as well be a stone idol on a mountain-top or a massive alien spaceship that has invaded earth. To discover, therefore, that Washington is a real place, that it has punk bands and Ethiopian taxi drivers and crack dealers of unrivalled boldness and persistence, comes as a pleasant surprise.

Yet as I lay on that bed, alone in that room, watching a curious cockroach dart in and out of the broken rubbish bag, the White House Hostel could have been an abandoned orbital space station. All at once I found myself with a yearning familiar to anyone who has ever spent any time on the road: the need for a friend.

As if on cue, the Norwegian made his entry. 'I think I am also slippy,' he said as he closed the door behind him. 'I am tired like a working dog.'

Fate is a sinkhole. Into it we fall and are drawn inexorably together. There is no fighting fortune's centrifuge. Of all the beds in the eight rooms of the White House Hostel, what were the chances that the Norwegian had, that morning, been assigned the one next to mine? As he spread out in his bunk, propping his head on his hand, I was filled with an uneasy premonition.

The conversation resumed. I was quizzed about my travels and my plans for the future. My responses were less than generous. I wanted to sleep but, crippled by politeness, allowed him to continue his interrogation.

'And do you have brothers and sees-ters?' he asked.

As the eldest of nine, this is not a question I like to answer, an honest response invariably acting as an invitation to various amateur comedians, convinced of their originality, to give their take on the sex lives of my parents, coupled with hilarious observations on the benefits of television ownership and/or enquiries into the nature of my family's religious beliefs. But that didn't worry me now. The personal turn of this conversation heralded an uncomfortable new note of intimacy. My unease grew and began to take shape. Against my better instincts I answered his question.

'Eight! Hoo hoo hoo,' he chortled, shifting up on his arm and coyly cocking his head in my direction. 'My, my,' he said. 'And are they all as prit-ee as you?'

I groaned internally, not so much from disgust as from my own naivety. How had I not seen this coming? What part of the trail of clues starting with a Jackie Kennedy teaspoon and ending with a locked door, a sly smile and a bulging fanny pack had I missed? Perhaps at the age of twenty-one I had simply assumed that people of a certain age just didn't have sex. Maybe I was too unworldly to realise that the inclinations of a man who pulled herring from the frozen northern oceans would be anything but heterosexual. Whatever the cause of my obliviousness, I was not to have long to ponder.

With a single motion, more elegant and sprightly than I would have given him credit for, the Norwegian rose from the bed and launched himself across the room. In less than a second, the full force of his considerable bulk was upon me, his hands pinning my shoulders to the bed, the trunks of his thighs gripping my own in a vice of muscle. A series of frantic crotch thrusts quickly followed, accompanied by a rain of slobbering kisses with all the tender eroticism of a bulldog drinking from a bowl. My protests were ignored as the thrusting doubled in speed. Then, staring into my eyes with an expression of almost childish anticipation, he leaned into my ear and whispered a phrase that over the years I have often pondered and yet am still no closer to fully understanding, 'Did you made it?'

Getting laid while travelling is a common fantasy. Indeed, it is probably a very large portion of the motive for travel itself. I am not immune to these daydreams. I have whiled away many a dreary bus journey hoping that some doe-eyed Eduardo or Yusef would board, take the seat next to mine, then announce in halting English that he wished to take me back to his village and make rough love to me on the skin of an animal he had recently slaughtered. Such scenes are among the stock clichés of travel literature. In reality, of course, nobody ever meets anybody travelling. There are no stolen kisses at midnight by a Venetian canal. No pacts to meet atop a skyscraper in a year's time. I can guarantee you'll never sit next to anyone on an airplane who's worth sharing an armrest with, let alone bodily fluids.

The notion that if we travel enough we may one day bump into the love of our lives is nothing more than a cruel fantasy invented by publishing companies looking to sell books by deranged divorcees with over-mortgaged Tuscan villas. And as I lay pinned under this enormous, panting Scandinavian, kicking like an upturned cockroach, it occurred to me that this was probably the closest I would ever come to a real holiday romance. With every thrust, the cruel realities of being on the other side of the world and without a friend seemed closer and sharper than ever.

It would be too liberal a definition of the word to describe the acts perpetrated upon me by the Norwegian as 'rape'. After a valiant struggle and several demands to be freed he eventually returned to his own quarters where he lay for some minutes, coyly masturbating in what seemed a state of genuine bemusement; clearly he regarded the incident as little more than some unfortunate cross-cultural etiquette breach, as if he had forgotten to remove his shoes indoors or dipped his chopsticks in the communal food bowl. And who knew: perhaps it was. There is a possibility that such behaviour was not uncommon in his part of the world, that in the Norwegian fishing community to retreat to a bedroom with a strange man and engage in conversation about your family is code for, 'Yes, I would like to make love to you with my pants on.' Assessing my options I stood up, wiped a silvery trail from the front of my jeans and retreated downstairs to see if I could make alternative sleeping arrangements.

An appeal for help to the staff of the White House Hostel was, in retrospect, a doomed gesture. It wasn't only the residents who were pushing the boundaries of sanity; while not as actively unbalanced as many of the guests, the employees and management were notably odd, bordering on downright creepy. Most notable was the hostel's owner, a figure referred to only as 'Tito', who lived in a single room by the toilets on the top floor at the end of a long corridor. From this chamber Tito controlled the entire operation, communicating by a series of vicious orders barked through the partially open door.

'Wardell, have you cleaned the goddamn kitchen? Wardell … *Wardell!* Get down there and clean that fucking kitchen, goddamn it. I am not gonna ask you again, cunt!'

Tito never emerged from his room. The most I saw of him was a small pair of chubby feet in white sports socks, the soles turned grey from dirt, stretched out on a pink bedspread.

In time, this faceless, disembodied figure took on in my mind an almost mythic quality—a sort of Great Oz figure—an impression only enhanced by the booming commands emanating from the bedroom. 'Wardell! Wardell! What did I say, you fucking asshole? Clean the goddamn kitchen or I'm gonna get down and knock the black outta ya.'

Wardell seemed to be the manager of the hostel and, I supposed, its cleaner—although, judging by the state of the facilities, an understandably unenthusiastic one. He was of average height and weight but had a big, womanly bottom that ground together when he walked, like a fat mouth eating. His hair lay in smooth, kinky waves across his scalp and was slashed to one side with a vicious part. He spoke with a soft lisp, making everything he said sound sexually suggestive, an effect heightened by his constant rearrangement of his substantial package.

'Do you think these jeans are too tight?' he would ask, running his hands slowly over his hips. 'Some folks say I got a big butt. I just say, "More cushion for the pushin."' He gave a tittering laugh, holding his fingers to his mouth like a shy Japanese schoolgirl.

Most of Wardell's time seemed to be spent sitting on the brown couch in the TV room. Occasionally we would watch TV together and, sometimes, by the dim light of a hockey game or a rerun of *Laverne and Shirley*, I would catch him staring. When our eyes met, he would wipe at the spit in the corners of his mouth with a delicate pinkie finger before painting his lips with his tongue.

The hostel's alleged 24-hour receptionist was Marco, a French backpacker who was working at the White House in return for a dorm bed—the standard of his accommodation reflecting the amount of work he did, which is to say next to none. Of all the staff, Marco was by far the easiest to get along with. Partial to delivering long, oddly soothing monologues in a heavy accent, he spent most of the day sitting in his room smoking endless joints by a crack in an open window. With slow, considered breaths he blew the smoke into the snowstorm outside only to watch, impassively, as it blew back in, bringing with it a small flurry of snowflakes. A contradictory character, Marco somehow managed to combine open-minded tolerance and mellow geniality with a brand of condescending racism popular among the French.

'Black people, zay are very free,' he would say, leaning into the window to exhale the smoke from a roach gripped between a pair of tweezers. 'Zay are more in touch wis zeir emo-shuns. Zay feel diply about sings. A black man doesn't sink so much about ze con-see-quances of 'eez ack-shuns. 'E just acts! Zis is why zay can be so vy-o-lant. But you should re-maim-bah—it eez not zair folt. Zay are like chil-drun—free and wild, like zee arni-marls on ze plains of ze Seren-gat-ee.'

The only other staff member at the White House was Leroy. He came from his apartment down the road every day and seemed to be the only person who did any work.

'You lazy bitches,' he would moan, running a vacuum cleaner vigorously across the floor. 'Sittin' round watchin' goddamn *Melrose Place* while Leroy picks up all your fuckin' Snickers wrappers and your ramen noodles and condoms. Move your fuckin' feet, goddamn it. Don't worry, you can go back to watching your beautiful white people fuck one another as soon as Leroy been done servin' you, masser.'

Leroy was black, in his late forties, and always referred to himself in the third person. Tall and very thin, he had swishy expressive hands and wrists like wooden spoons, each encircled by half a dozen golden bangles that tinkled and clanked as he cleaned or gesticulated with disgust at the population of the TV room.

'Fuckin' disgustin' is what it is. Think Leroy wants to do this shit? Think he's got nothin' better do? Think he couldn't be out enjoyin' his-self? Think he couldn't be down at the club stickin' dollar bills in some chicken's underpants? Mm-hm. That's right—Leory is in a bad fuckin' mood today. Motherfuckers better watch it.'

Despite the frequency and volubility of his complaints, Leroy was a generous man with a greater interest in the welfare of the hostel's residents than any of the other employees. He also knew everything about everyone at The White House, both employees and residents, and was not shy about sharing gossip on subjects ranging from the hostel's dubious financial arrangements to its violation of safety codes. From Leroy I had learned that the White House had once been the subject of a short television news item after one of its foreign guests was stabbed in the neck while buying drugs. One morning he took me outside and proudly showed me the bloodstain on the pavement.

Leroy's favourite topic was the sex lives of the hostel's management and residents. The details were graphic and shared without prompting, all punctuated by expressive rattles of his bangles. Together with Marco, he would sit for hours, smoking hash and discussing the latest scandalous couplings: threesomes in the TV room; foursomes in the showers; a spit roast on the porch. To listen to Leroy, the White House Hostel was the last days of Nero with bunk beds.

Upstairs, the pair was engaged in their evening ritual of smoke and gossip. I sat down but was not offered any of the nearly extinct joint. Marco drew on the tiny butt as if trying to lift a bowling ball with his lips. While they were on the subject, it seemed a good time to raise my own problems with the Norwegian.

'Goddamn—Leroy knew it!' he screeched when I told him what had happened. 'He didn't fool Leroy with all that butch shit. The moment he stepped through the door, Leroy knew he was in the life.'

I told him I needed another room.

'Sorry, man,' said Marco, lighting another pre-rolled jay. 'Zair iz no ozzer room. We are all fool, one 'undred pro-cent.'

I protested: surely there was something they could do? 'Can you move him or kick him out? Maybe ask Tito for me.'

'Huh, Tito!' Leroy exclaimed, taking the jay from Marco and inhaling sharply. 'Don't tell Tito, unless you wanna get it from both ends. That asshole is into some devious motherfuckin' shit. He will fuck *anything*. And by anything I mean that freak Wardell.'

'Oh yeah, eez troo, man,' added Marco. 'Ee doon't care. Poo-see, ass … 'e don' give a shit. Once ah fund 'im fucking zis 'omeless guy oo leaves on ze stoop. Ze naxt day, ze guy 'ad a new jaquet from ze lost and foond.'

'Look,' said Leroy, 'there ain't a room in the whole of DC. It's almost New Year's, man. What's he gonna do? He can't rape you while there's other people in the room. Just keep your eyes on your fries and sleep with your jeans on.'

As Leroy exhaled out the window, a little flurry of snow-flakes settled on the floor.

For the rest of my time at the White House Hostel I was as chaste as a harem girl in the court of the sultan, my life a careful regime of bathroom quick-changes, sleeping pressed against the wall and the constant company of chaperones. It didn't do much good. The next morning I rolled over, peeled open a cautious eye and was immediately confronted by the sight of the Norwegian vigorously masturbating, an inviting smile on his large pink face.

How long had he been going before I woke? An hour? Half an hour? Had he even slept? I wiped the grit from my eyes and looked around the room. The rest of the bunks in the dormitory remained still and quiet. Bodies lay like emergent pupae in sleeping bags or wrapped in a mummy's shroud of sheets, feet twitching, chests rising and falling with a soft accordion wheeze, the rhythm punctuated only by a sudden flatulent exclamation.

From the bed across the room the Norwegian stared into my eyes, licking invisible frosting from his lips. Sheets pulled back, he worked at his monstrous gourd with the slow, exaggerated gestures of one forcing the last, difficult pumps into a bicycle tyre. Outside, the ceaseless snow fell by the window. I would not leave today.

As I gathered my things, I did my best to ignore the Norwegian. My irritation was only exacerbated by the events of the previous evening. Stumbling home in the early hours, drunk and disoriented in the dimly lit corridors, I had turned left instead of right and found myself in the room of the demented Japanese bra-thrower. Like a reanimated corpse, she sat bolt upright, her hair fanned about her face. 'Is it your bed?' she screamed. I assured her it wasn't, but as I made my retreat into the corridor she followed.

Outside her room we stood for a moment, facing one another. In the light her face was deathly pale. Without warning she lunged towards me. I took a step back; she took another forward, slicing at me with what I quickly realised was a small box-cutter. With lightning strokes she drew jagged Zs through the air, imitating the sound of a blade cutting through flesh. 'Tsst! Tsst!' she hissed, following me to my room. Once inside, I slammed the door. She made no effort to enter, but for the next twenty minutes I stood with my ear pressed against the wood, listening as she prowled outside, slashing the razor and threatening phantoms.

In the dim morning light it all seemed like a bad dream. Making it clear to the Norwegian that I wasn't in the mood to reprise my role as camp whore, I retreated to the bathroom. After changing in two inches of stagnant water, I grabbed my coat from the room—the Norwegian offering a final flash of pink cucumber—and made my escape.

That morning Washington's charms were wearing thin. Here it was: New Year's Eve and my only date was a Scandinavian pervert with a collection of ornamental teaspoons. At least, I consoled myself, I had managed to avoid Edward. As I descended the stairs I imagined him wandering the streets of Washington, a white ghost in a white landscape, looking for someone else to haunt.

'Morning,' said Edward, blinking at me from the velvet sofa.

My heart sank.

'Where are you going?' he asked.

For a moment I stammered, trying to remember somewhere he had already been. Edward stared at me expectantly—rugged up in his hat, gloves and coat, he looked like a child waiting for his estranged father's access visit excursion to the zoo.

I like to think that I make an effort to be kind and polite. In fact, at times, my politeness verges on a crippling, masochistic neurosis. I am aware, however, that a vast majority of this lock-jawed civility stems not from any human compassion so much as a desire to avoid social discomfort. Confronted now with Edward, his imploring eyes, there seemed no other choice.

'You can't come with me today, Edward,' I said. The words seem to come from an unfamiliar place, as if I were controlled by a higher power, the puppet of some cruel crusher of dreams.

'Oh, okay.' His face had that same impassive quality of a fish staring back through an aquarium. 'Then we can go out tonight.'

For a moment I recanted it all: I had been too harsh; Edward shared little but had I really made any effort to get to know him? Briefly I entertained images of the fun we might have had: Edward and me at the Air and Space Museum, planting a flag on the moon; the pair of us hunched over a roleplaying game, spinning a twenty-sided die before giddily celebrating our acquisition of an invisibility cloak; strolling hand in hand across a glassy beach.

'No, I'm sorry,' I said. 'I'm meeting some other friends.'

The lie was utterly transparent. I hated myself as soon as I'd said it.

'Oh, okay,' he said, his expression unchanged.

There was a silence broken only by the sound of the lunatic in the corner muttering curses into his Bible.

'See you later, Edward,' I said as I made my way down the stairs and into the snowy street, alone.

———

Despite the extreme cold and constant snow, a day without Edward was total liberation. After spending a warming day at the National Gallery, I headed back to hostel, where I found Leroy handing out invitations to a New Year's Day party.

'You can come too, Crocodile Dundee,' he said, handing me a small strip of paper with an address written on it in pink ink. 'Leroy lives just round the corner and it's traditional for him to cook soul food every New Year's Day for you filthy, cheap-ass *motherfuckers.*'

New Year's Eve turned out to be much better than expected. After hooking up with a Swede from the next room, I headed out and quickly became staggeringly drunk, not arriving home until some time near 5 a.m.

In the cruel light of morning, memories came like shameful evidence photos in the police interrogation room of my conscience: dancing shirtless with the Swede on stage at an Ethiopian restaurant; being thrown out of a nightclub after stroking the bartender's afro suggestively; making a half-hearted pass at the Swede after my introduction to Jell-O shots, which I could still taste when I opened my eyes and looked about the room, the daylight like knives in my eyeballs.

It was almost midday. The Norwegian and Edward were nowhere to be seen. The smell in the dormitory was of warm road kill.

After pulling on my clothes, I crept cautiously downstairs and stuck my head into the common room. Marco was sprawled on the couch watching an episode of *Oprah*.

'Morning,' I said. 'Is there anyone else about?'

Marco looked at me with red eyes. He had clearly not been to bed. 'Why eez eet on zees shoe zat zee ow-dience eez alwayz clappink for Oprah? She iss like a modern shaman, conn-acted to zee spee-ret of zer jangle.'

Roused from the couch with the promise of a spliff at Leroy's place, he followed me downstairs into the snow-covered streets.

When we arrived at Leroy's apartment, the party was just starting, a sudden rush of guests swelling the numbers. In the tiny kitchen the atmosphere was hot and convivial. With Leroy flouring the chicken and chopping vegetables there was a genuine sense of intimacy and camaraderie. People told jokes and compared stories of their travels. Friendly arguments erupted. After three months on the road alone, I finally felt, for a moment, the familiar warmth of belonging.

While we drank wine and waited for the food, conversation turned to hostel gossip. Wardell, we learned, had not returned from New Year's. 'Somebody needs to check the sling at Manacle,' called Leroy over the sound of chopping. 'Bitch may need some keys.'

Soon, everyone started complaining about their roommates. The Japanese lunatic had obviously been busy in her campaign of terror: one girl had come back after a day out to find the jeans she had hung up to dry cut to ribbons.

'That bitch is motherfuckin' crazy,' said Leroy. 'In fact, she's probably fuckin' Tito right now.' The room laughed as he continued chopping vegetables. 'But give Leroy her any day over that motherfuckin' freak in your room.'

I thought for a moment. 'Which one?'

'The one with those thick glasses and that sad-ass motherfuckin' face. Redneck freak gives Leroy the motherfuckin' creeps. Get yo ass back on the Greyhound to Tennessee, my friend.'

I was confused. 'You mean the short guy with the white blond hair?'

'Yes, Crocodile Dundee, what did Leroy just say to you? The redneck motherfucker in your room. Your goddamn best friend.'

I paused. It seemed strange Leroy could have made so elemental a mistake as to think that Edward was white. Was this, I wondered, some obscure black cultural matter? I hesitated for a moment, aware that I was on uncertain ground.

'Well, he's kind of odd,' I said. 'But he's not a redneck. Actually, he's not even white. He's a black albino, and he's from New Jersey.'

'Excuse me?' said Leroy, using a rare personal pronoun.

I repeated myself.

'What you talkin' 'bout, asshole? He ain't no black albino. Trust me, Leroy knows black albinos and he knows rednecks. And that is a motherfuckin' honky.'

It was difficult for me to believe what I was hearing. 'Look, I'm sorry,' I said, suddenly aware that everyone in the room was listening, 'but he's not white. I just shared a room with him for a week. He's an albino—trust me.'

Leroy's look was one of shock. For a moment he stared about him, his plucked eyebrows arched, as if he needed confirmation that he wasn't hearing things. His gaze settled back on me. 'You think Leroy don't know a goddamn albino when he sees one?' He waggled the knife as he spoke, his tone becoming high and affronted. 'Now you listen, man. Leroy is telling you what he is: he is white. White as vanilla ice cream. White as yo' momma's white ass. A goddamn motherfuckin' *cracker*.'

I was wary of how charged the atmosphere had become. In race-obsessed America—where my father only narrowly avoided being torn limb from limb by patrons of a Harlem diner in the late 1970s after ordering a 'white coffee'—we were venturing into dangerous territory. At this point, most people would have conceded the argument, let him have the victory. But this was not a race issue; this was a me-being-right-and-Leroy-being-wrong issue, and I was damned if I was going to let a little thing like 300 years of systematic racial oppression and ethnic tension get in the way.

'He is not white,' I said, each word separate and distinct. 'He is a black albino.'

Leroy glared, his eyes growing to golf balls in their sockets. In his right hand he was still holding the knife. 'Go to the goddamn liquor store, motherfucker!' he yelled, slicing the knife through the air, first towards me and then towards the door. 'And get some more booze right now! More alcohol is the only way Leroy is gonna be able to cope with your goddamn, ignorant, motherfuckin', know-it-all, Crocodile Dundee ass.'

For a moment he just stared, the air whistling through his nose. It occurred to me that he might be about to stick the knife in my back when I turned.

'Whatchoo waitin' for?' he screamed, stabbing at me again. 'Go on, motherfucker—scat! Before I give y'all lesson about who is and isn't a goddamn nigger in this town.'

'I'll calm wiz you,' said Marco sleepily.

Outside the weather was still bitter, but the snow had stopped. Patches of grey sludge, like melted Styrofoam, made the pavements treacherous. The streets were empty of traffic. I realised I would be able to leave tomorrow.

'Doon worry 'bout Leroy, man,' said Marco. 'Ze blacks are passion-ot people. Especially when zay are defending zair tribe.'

As we walked I ruminated on my argument with Leroy. To some degree I felt ashamed of having spoiled the good mood of the party. To a much larger degree I felt Leroy could go fuck himself. I was tired of him; sick of his ghetto bitch routine all performed for the benefit of a room of white foreigners, eager for a taste of his exoticism. As I walked the slippery streets I fumed at the injustice of it all. Deep down, however, I knew that my anger stemmed not from having been wronged but rather the sense of being back where I had started, friendless and isolated, the over-whelming loneliness as cold and comfortless as the piles of slush on the streets.

Our journey to the liquor store continued one cautious step at a time. Suddenly, Marco stopped in the street and pressed a hand on my chest.

'Zair he is,' he said, pointing an astonished finger into the distance.

'Who?'

'Zee guy. Zee rayd-nack from your rheum.'

I looked across the street. At his own stilted pace, his neck brace a fleshy plinth for his head, the Galapagos tortoise shuffled down the footpath. On his face, a previously unseen accessory: a pair of thick-lensed glasses almost identical to Edward's.

The mystery solved, Marco and I laughed and watched as he disappeared into the distance, licking at the faint ring of orange about his mouth.

'Ah yes,' said Marco. 'I noo zee man you are talk-ink about. Yes, 'ee iss a black al-been-oo.' He shook his head mournfully. 'Ah, eez vary sat—traj-eek!—when a man iss black in 'eez art but white on 'eez skeen. Ow can 'e ree-zolve zee ee-ner arni-maal wis zee camoo-flage of ceevil-eyes-ay-shun?'

After buying the wine we made our way back to the apartment. As we walked, anger and frustration gave way to elation and contentedness. How happy I was to be going back to Leroy's: I would be the Prodigal Son returned, welcomed into the fold to bathe in the warm glow of fried chicken and friendship. As the freezing air stung my cheeks and burned my scalp it seemed to take my hangover with it.

At the apartment I barged straight through the door, excited, like a dog clutching a dead bird in its jaws. 'Guess what?' I said, cheerfully addressing my fellow guests. 'It's all been a big mistake. We were talking about two separate guys. The one in my room is definitely a black albino.'

Leroy nodded, his expression queasy and distracted. Silently, he turned and busied himself with a plate of fried chicken. As the clanking of his golden bangles filled room, I became aware of a terrible silence. I turned to see Edward. For a moment he stared, the hurt in his grey eyes unmis-takable. Slowly his white, almost translucent, lids closed in defeat. His head nodded towards the floor.

Immediately I felt my face grow hot. I stared about at the stony, disapproving faces. Beside Edward, the Norwegian smiled, locking eyes with me triumphantly as he laid a comforting hand on his new friend's shoulder.

Mr and Mrs Kumar Make a Plan

Mr and Mrs Kumar were happy to meet us. More than happy. 'Oh, praise be to God!' called Mr Kumar raising his arms to the sky and rocking our rowboat on the Ganges. 'Praise be that he should have delivered you to us! You, a professional writer and journalist for the newspapers! Oh, praise be!' Mr Kumar lowered his hands and joined them in prayer before his face, his fingers bisecting his eyes. 'This is truly a happy day. You have been sent here to help me—to help me with my children! You will see to it that they go to a good university and you will help me take them to Australia where they will get the education they deserve. Oh, thank you, God.' With a graceful motion Mr Kumar bowed before me, returned his hands to his lap and beamed, a sparkle of tears in his eyes. Behind him, Mrs Kumar merely sniffed, fixing me with an expectant expression from behind thick glasses. For the first, but not the last, time in my brief but intense relationship with the Kumars, I would have reason to suspect that between who I was and who they thought I was there might be some discrepancy.

My friend Carrie and I had met Mr and Mrs Kumar the previous evening while looking for a Mexican restaurant.

It seemed strange, the idea of a Mexican restaurant in India's holiest city—like finding a Starbucks in the Vatican. Compared to the rest of our week in Varanasi, however— a week in which we had narrowly avoided being killed in a cattle stampede, had our faces rubbed by the bloodied stumps of a leper's hands, seen a rotting human corpse prised free from the shore with a stick, been attacked by wild pigs and beaten over the head with swords during an Islamic fundamentalist riot—the Mexican restaurant and our subsequent meeting with the Kumars seemed an oasis of gentle domesticity within the Hieronymus Bosch Variety Hour that constituted daily life in the city.

'Come in! Come in!' cried Mr Kumar, clearly delighted that we had made good on our promise to return after our meal.

I handed him a plastic bag of sticky Indian pastries we had brought as a gift. Mr Kumar took the bag and stared at it as one might a flaming bag of dog faeces. 'We are not eating these,' he said, and handed the bag to Mrs Kumar, who disappeared into the kitchen.

The Kumars' home was a concrete box on a dusty back-street near the main train station. The filth was exceptional. Inside, the walls were speckled with mould. The dingy kitchen and bathroom, glimpsed behind heavy, dirt-matted curtains, were a sooty shambles. Every now and then a whiff of sewage would fill the air before quickly dissipating.

The main living area consisted of a cramped all-purpose living room furnished with a few rickety wooden chairs and a small circular table. A row of bookcases divided the room, partially obscuring a bed with a purple cover. The shelves were filled with old kitchen utensils and dusty stacks of the *Times of India* tied up in yellowing bundles.

Behind the bed, against the back wall, was another table, this one piled with more stacks of newspapers, the financial sections removed and placed in smaller piles beside them. An enormous antiquated air-conditioning unit, its straw filter broken and spilling out, filled the rest of the table, the entire still life covered in a volcanic layer of grey dust.

It looked less like a home than the jungle headquarters of some outlaw guerrilla group—appropriate considering that, for the next twenty-four hours, we would be their captives.

'Sit down, sit down,' commanded Mr Kumar. As we perched ourselves on the chairs, Mrs Kumar emerged with tea and sweets before retreating to other side of the room to sit in silence.

'We had an Australian friend once before,' said Mr Kumar, pulling out a photo album. 'His name was Peter. Oh, what a gala time we had! Funny and generous. Oh, so generous.' Mr Kumar opened the album to reveal a series of pictures of the younger Kumars, the images turned blue with age. The photos had been taken in a garden. The Kumars could be seen smiling and standing by a tall, bearded Australian wearing flares and a floral shirt, curly blond hair falling to his shoulders. Beside him, the tiny, pudgy couple looked like theme-park tourists posing by a suited cartoon character. 'Oh, what a gala time,' said Mr Kumar.

On the next page was a series of photos taken the same day, featuring an almost unrecognisable Mrs Kumar lounging on the grass in front of a rosebush. With one hand propping up her head, her hair cascading across a bosom barely contained by a tight floral sari, there was a hint of the Bollywood temptress about her. This suggestiveness was made slightly incongruous by her squat figure and a pair of black square-framed glasses so enormous they seemed to consume half her face. Behind them, her pupils were dark bovine saucers, her eyebrows a pair of Jurassic caterpillars.

'My wife,' said Mr Kumar, with an unexpected hint of lasciviousness. From the distant corner, in her self-imposed exile, Mrs Kumar acknowledged our compliments with a few brisk nods then returned her gaze to her lap to run her hands along the creases in her sari.

At their insistence, we arranged to meet the Kumars before dawn the next morning, our last day in Varanasi. Unfortunately, hungover and disoriented by the dark labyrinth of the city's streets, we quickly became lost. By the time we found them they had been waiting half an hour.

'We told you where to go,' scolded Mr Kumar as he led us to the boat he had hired.

'We're very sorry,' I said, alarmed by his vehemence. 'We walked to the wrong ghat.'

Mr Kumar paused and assessed my face, like some all-powerful monarch considering whether to have me interred alive in concrete. 'It is no matter,' he said, the grim mouth suddenly melting into a smile of patriarchal mercy. 'Get in the boat.'

As we got into the river the rosy tints of the morning were almost gone. The sky was a dull yellow and the water grey, almost purple, flecked by the orange fires of the funeral pyres. In the flames the bodies burned ceaselessly, sending a rich slick of oily ash, rotten flowers and glittery fabric into the river. Around us the other tourist boats bobbed and turned as their occupants strained for long-lens shots of the cremations. From the stone tiers lining the shore, pilgrims were wading into the river, washing themselves and offering prayers to the rising sun: old men in ill-fitting underpants, stark-naked sadhus with elaborate face-painting, middle-aged women in layered saris and, in the midst of it all, a pale Japanese boy in bright board shorts, his arms wrapped tightly around his chest as he stood up to his knees, staring apprehensively into the filthy water.

With a dismissive flick of his wrist, Mr Kumar signalled that we should return to shore. As the oarsman dug into the water a white island of swollen flesh nudged the prow then continued its slow journey down the river. 'A cow,' said Mrs Kumar, blinking behind her huge glasses.

Back on land a typical day in Varanasi was unfolding: a sadhu, naked but for a covering of blue paint, walked through a children's cricket match, his dreadlocks sweeping the ground; an ascetic crabbed on his hands up the steps of the ghat, his legs withered to tangled roots from his renunciation of walking; a delirious man who had been drinking water from the river paced up and down by the bank, shivering and vomiting convulsively.

As we walked, Mr Kumar asked us questions, mostly about our parents and our education. I hesitated to answer truthfully lest the information further expand his already inflated view of me.

'A political journalist!' cried Mr Kumar. He paused and stared at me with Christmas-morning eyes. 'Your father is a political journalist? A man who writes about politics and the government, izzit?'

'Yes.'

'In the capital city, izzit?'

'Yes.'

Mr Kumar raised his hands to the sky and chanted a prayer of thanks. Carrie and I swapped covert looks of alarm.

Our journey along the ghats continued. To my surprise, the normally mute Mrs Kumar assumed the guiding duties. As we walked she pointed to temples and other items of interest, explaining each with a few staccato lines, haiku-like in their brevity: 'The temple is old; the people here are from the south'; 'Lepers come to Varanasi; some will be dead soon'; 'That cow is dying; its stomach has fallen from its body.'

Eventually we arrived at a wooden temple on the Lalita Ghat. 'A gift from Nepal,' said Mrs Kumar. 'It has influence from Chinese.'

The temple was very beautiful, its pagoda roofs and natural colours a relief from the fleshy pinks and acid primaries that dominated Varanasi. The beams and doors were all covered in intricate carvings, many of which, on closer inspection, proved to be wildly sexual. 'Here is erotic,' said Mrs Kumar, pointing to a copulating couple, their bodies arched backwards into an obscene approximation of the McDonald's arches. 'And here.' She pointed to a male figure who, either out of ignorance or a misguided spirit of experimentation, appeared to be stabbing his erection into the top of a woman's head.

'Erotic,' said Mrs Kumar, her enormous glasses close to our faces as we peered at a couple in a wheelbarrow posture.

'Erotic … erotic … erotic.'

After a short auto-rickshaw ride—and a brief tussle with a herd of wild pigs—the four us arrived back at the Kumars' home. In the morning light it looked even dirtier and more depressing than it had the previous evening. Mrs Kumar emerged from the kitchen with tea and a tray of sweets and placed them on the table. I watched as on the other side of the room a rat played peekaboo behind a pile of newspapers.

We drank the tea and ate the sweets and Mrs Kumar once again retreated to the far end of the room. Sitting on the bed she watched us with her huge owl eyes, her bare feet swinging gently to agitate the cheap purple throw.

'So,' said Mr Kumar, smiling and leaning forward eagerly in his seat, 'you are a journalist, izzit?'

'Well, yes. Of a sort.'

'And yet you studied the history of art?'

'Yes.'

'I see,' said Mr Kumar. He pressed his fingertips into a spire, like a Bond villain. 'And you did not want to study computers or business?'

'No.'

Dropping his hands to his side, Mr Kumar thought for a moment. He had the look of a man who had arrived at a tricky diplomatic impasse, as if I had just revealed I was a communist or had once spent time in prison for child molestation. Eventually he brought his hands back to his chin. 'Tell me,' he said, 'how my children can study at university in Australia.'

I was hesitant but did my best to explain the process, adding that it was potentially expensive and complicated but not unusual. If Mr Kumar's children wanted to study in Australia, I concluded, it might not be out of their reach.

'And the forms? You can obtain them for me?'

'What forms, Mr Kumar?'

'The university entrance forms!' he bellowed.

Mr Kumar's plan to send his children to Australia had obviously been the subject of much thought, little of it especially useful. He seemed to have no particular reason for wishing his children to study in Australia, as opposed to anywhere else, and he had almost no conception of what life was like in a western city: on several occasions he was to make earnest enquiries into the number and value of our cattle holdings and was convinced that he would be able to purchase a farm within easy commuting distance to a city campus. His central obsession, however, was with forms and brochures, which he craved with an intensity more usually associated with late-stage heroin addiction. Any attempt to convince him that these had been made almost wholly redundant by the internet revolution, and that he could simply download everything he needed from a nearby cyber cafe, was pointless: Mr Kumar had the Indian's talismanic faith in the power of paperwork and efforts to persuade him otherwise were treated with the same air of oblivious disregard as the constant traffic outside.

For the next hour our conversation followed the same pattern: Mr Kumar insisting that I post him forms and brochures; me trying to convince him they were unnecessary; Mr Kumar ignoring me as he wrote lists of tasks to be completed on my return home, including an estimate of the cost of a modest farm and small herd of cattle.

In the lulls of this absurd exchange we learned something of his family. The Kumars had three children, two boys and a girl, all three studying IT or business at universities across the country. Their phone numbers were presented to us along with details of their educational histories. When we asked if they would have arranged marriages he made a face and slipped his palms together, as if wiping away dirt. 'Snick, snack,' he said. 'It is all done.'

Of the three, the one for whom Mr Kumar seemed to nurse the most hope was his daughter, Meena. 'Ah, my daughter!' he cried, presenting us a photo of a bundled infant, her face daubed in caste marks. 'She is being the top two percentile. Currently she is studying in Bangalore, in Electronic City—Electronic City! But soon she will study in Australia. Here, allow me to write down her address. When you go to Bangalore to talk to her about study it will be easier to be making contact.'

As Mr Kumar wrote his daughter's details in a careful script I took the opportunity to announce our departure. Thanking the couple for their hospitality, we began to make our excuses.

'We were hoping to see the Man Singh Observatory before we left,' said Carrie, by way of explanation.

'Ah, but I can take you there!' cried Mr Kumar. 'There is no need for you to worry. After that we will return here and have lunch.'

'What do you like to eat?' said Mrs Kumar, making an unexpected cameo from across the room.

'Oh no, really,' I said. 'We couldn't.'

'Do you like tandoor?' asked Mr Kumar. 'Of course you do! You will have tandoor chicken.'

Rising from her position on the bed, Mrs Kumar scurried into the kitchen.

'Oh no, we couldn't,' I said.

'Do not be worrying, my friends. When we return from our sightseeing you will be enjoying a delicious authentic Indian meal. What a gala time we will have. But first,' he said, handing us the book in which he had been writing, 'you must write down your full names and addresses as well as your educational qualifications and the names of your parents and their addresses and educational qualifications. Then we will establish the best way for you to organise the education of my children in Australia.'

I took a bite of my sweet, but all I could taste was sticky dust.

The three of us rode in uncomfortable proximity in the back of an auto-rickshaw. As we moved through the streets of suburban Varanasi, Mr Kumar spoke of our itinerary. 'First we will be seeing the university and the observatory,' he said, punctuating his monologue with shouted instructions to the driver. 'Then the silk factory. You know of course that Varanasi silk is being the most famous in all the world! And the prices I will get for you—oh, the prices you will not be believing!'

This latest development made us nervous. 'I don't think we really want to buy any silk, Mr Kumar,' cried Carrie over the roar of the auto-rickshaw. Mr Kumar just looked at her, smiled broadly and nodded in the manner of someone who is humouring a cretin.

After a short ride we arrived in the shabby courtyard of a university complex; it appeared to be deserted.

'This is Benares Hindu University,' announced Mr Kumar, alighting from the rickshaw. 'This is one of India's premium institutions of higher learning. We will be taking some time to look here because, unfortunately, the observatory is closed.'

'But in the guidebook it says it's open until five every day,' protested Carrie.

'This is incorrect,' said Mr Kumar with an air of finality. 'I am being very reliably informed by the driver that it is currently closed. But look, see—we have many interesting buildings of historical importance to view here.'

The buildings of the campus were modern and unremarkable. Nevertheless, we strolled about the deserted square for a few optimistic minutes, watched by a caretaker leaning on a broom. Sensing our apprehension, Mr Kumar signalled we should get back in the auto-rickshaw. I began to chafe at his bossiness. 'Mr Kumar,' I said with all the firmness I could muster, 'I want to go and see the observatory. Please, can you check with someone else to see if it is really closed?' As the auto-rickshaw revved up and took off, Mr Kumar simply cupped his ear with his hand and rocked his head in a gesture of theatrical frustration.

The silk factory was a warehouse in a field not far from the university. At the entrance the foreman greeted our host as an old friend. Down a corridor stained in *paan* spit we came to the workshops. In rooms of quite unnecessary dinginess a group of teenage boys sat on the floor at the centre of rickety wooden looms, each lit from above with a single bare bulb. Using their hands and feet the boys worked the levers and pulleys of the machines with the dexterity of cathedral organists, their spindly arachnid limbs moving at lightning pace. Compared to the boys the contraptions seemed enormous, as if the weavers had been swallowed by a strange mantrap—weird hybrid creatures enslaved by some alien power.

'The silk is cheap,' yelled Mr Kumar over the din, 'because the boys work for very little money.' He grinned at us with satisfaction and it took me a moment to realise he was boasting.

In a quieter room at the other end of the hall we sat barefoot on straw matting and were offered *paan* and tea in filthy plastic cups. The foreman appeared once more and with his younger assistants began to unroll countless bolts of fabric. For the next half-hour Mr Kumar cajoled us into buying. 'Can you believe it?' he screeched, fingering the silk before our faces. 'Look at the quality. And the prices … oh, the prices.' As we sat, several boys came and watched us through the doorway, squatting on their haunches and turning occasionally to spit red streaks of *paan* against the walls.

Eager to be gone, we each purchased a few pillowcases then asked Mr Kumar if we might leave. To our surprise he acquiesced immediately, clearing the doorway with dramatic swings of his arms, like a policeman at a riot. I felt he sensed in us a bigger prize.

Back at the Kumar residence, lunch was being laid out. By now we were ravenous and as Mrs Kumar placed the food before us we eyed the meal with anticipation. 'Oh, tandoor chicken!' cried Mr Kumar as Mrs Kumar disappeared to the other side of the room to sit, meal-less, on the end of the bed. 'You will never have tasted anything like it!'

From silver tiffin trays we ate lunch with our hands. The meal was a disappointment: the chicken a piece of thick red bark, the dhal a bowl of fragrant glue. Mrs Kumar's talents as a cook were, it seemed, roughly commensurate with her powers as a conversationalist. Nevertheless, with all the extravagant insincerity of parents at a school play, we praised her efforts, compliments she accepted with nothing more than a couple of brisk nods.

Watching her sit silently in the corner, as bored and indifferent as a film technician on set, I began to speculate on Mrs Kumar's role in all this. Was her passivity a cunning ploy, or was she secretly embarrassed by it all—her overbearing husband, her dirty home and bad cooking? I looked at the broken air-conditioning unit, imagined the hours of nagging, the passive-aggressive complaints about the heat; saw Mr Kumar arrive home one afternoon and dump the contraption on the table where it would sit for years, gathering dust. That day in the rose garden with their Australian friend, was this how she had imagined her future?

As we ate Mr Kumar continued a monologue on the brilliance of his children, their eventual education in Australia and our role in his plan, much of it annotated in his notebook. Pauses came only in the form of queries and demands, each with the expectation of a prompt and detailed response: 'Is $50,000 US dollars in cash sufficient to be purchasing a farm in Australia?'; 'What is the cost of rice?'; 'You will find for me the best course in computing and advise the cost of a year's tuition. Please obtain relevant forms.'

Resistance was futile. Mr Kumar was a brick wall to the forehead of reason. We could only do our best to answer his questions and count the minutes until we could leave.

Once tea had been poured and drunk we stood up and again announced our departure. 'We really must go, Mr Kumar,' I said. 'Our train leaves in a few hours and we still haven't bought tickets.'

'Oh, then we shall buy them for you!' cried Mr Kumar. He said something to his wife, who immediately began to ready herself for the journey to the station.

'No really, Mr Kumar,' said Carrie with a hint of distress. 'It's not necessary. We're very tired. We were up late. Please, we'll go now.'

'If you are tired, then you will be sleeping!' declared Mr Kumar. 'Please be taking our bed.'

Mrs Kumar raced over and began to rearrange the bed covers.

'Oh no, we couldn't,' we protested, as Mrs Kumar plumped the pillows.

'Get in the bed!' said Mr Kumar.

Hesitantly, under the couple's expectant gaze, we began to remove our shoes. Together we lay on top of the purple cover. The mattress was a cement slab under our backs but our eyes were heavy, our bodies exhausted. At the end of the bed the Kumars stood over us, watching as we lay frigidly side by side.

'Brendan,' whispered Carrie, 'I don't want to be here. I'm afraid.'

I was too, but what was to be done? The strange power the Kumars had over us was absolute. As Mr Kumar disappeared to the other side of the room, we stared at the constellations of mould on the ceiling. Suddenly, our tiredness grew overwhelming. My limbs seemed to disappear. As my eyelids drooped and my head began to nod, the overwhelming images of the day played on fast forward: the wild eyes of the vomiting man, the boys trapped in their machines, the relish with which Mrs Kumar had shown us those erotic sculptures.

I thought of the photos of the Kumars in the garden, the image of Mrs Kumar lying seductively among the roses. How did I get so tired? I remembered the food, the gluey dhal. What did drugs taste like? I tried to move but my body was too heavy. As sleep came I was aware of being watched.

'Sleep!' commanded Mr Kumar. 'Sleep … sleep.' We were unable to resist. From the other side of the room the huge bovine eyes of Mrs Kumar stared unblinking through her glasses.

Bangalore is probably the most orderly city in India, and Meena lived in the most orderly part of it. Electronic City is the centre of India's computer industry, a series of satellite towns about 30 kilometres from Bangalore proper. I arrived there, alone, almost three weeks after leaving Varanasi. Since that time, my strange afternoon with the Kumars had been relegated to a dim memory. The day had ended uneventfully: in defiance of my paranoid speculations there had been no robbery or somnolent molestations. After a seemingly never-ending series of farewells and confirmation that I would send Mr Kumar every necessary form or brochure, we had boarded our train and headed south.

Carrie had returned home early and, although I still had Meena's address and an Old Testament of written instructions from her father, a meeting with their daughter was not high on my list of priorities. Nevertheless, I had come to Bangalore. Why exactly, I could not say—there was almost nothing in the way of tourist sites and it represented a considerable detour from my intended route. My curiosity about Meena Kumar had obviously compelled me subconsciously, as if her father's hypnotic power controlled me even here.

The road to Electronic City is modern and congested. Office buildings clad in reflective glass line the highway, great piles of garbage festering in front. At one point we stopped by a mall under construction. The signs on the hoardings announced with heraldic triumph the international brands that would soon take up residency within— Subway, Levi's, Armani, Starbucks. Outside, a little girl approached the window of the taxi with an outstretched hand. She was very young and singing a low eerie chant that seemed oddly disconnected from her small body, as if she were channelling a spirit. When she turned, I saw that half her face was hideously disfigured; acid burns fell in a pink cascade from the top of her head to her chin. The scars looked recent: her hairless scalp was weeping, her left ear nothing but a smooth mound, a black hole at its centre. In shock I threw money at her. As the taxi took off I tried to repress the grotesque thought that someone had done it to her on purpose.

Down the highway at the entrance to Electronic City there were more convenient symbols of the new India. In the distance a huge pyramid of blue reflective glass rose up to the sky surrounded by teetering palm trees and a fence of barbed wire. Next to it stood an even more massive structure, a crystalline shard crisscrossed in reflective glass, its pointed tip like an alien craft preparing for take-off. As we drew nearer I could see the shantytowns of the immigrant workers ringing the perimeter, their houses made of cardboard and plastic sheeting, their children bathing in the open drains by the highway. As we drove by, a cow stared impassively, chewing a plastic bag.

After some searching in the empty industrial streets of Electronic City we eventually found Meena's university campus. It was a small exclusive computer-programming school run by one of the big Indian IT companies. Colleges like this received a million applications every year. For Meena to have been accepted, she must be very clever indeed.

At the guard's office I was ordered to state my business and fill out a visitor's book. Under name I wrote *Elvis Presley* and gave my address as *Gracelands*. The guard looked at the page, nodded solemnly, and ushered me into the complex. At the front desk I gave Meena's name to the receptionist and waited. After ten minutes, a small, astonished-looking girl in a floral sari and white plastic sandals with thick high heels arrived; with her squat frame, long hair and glasses she was the image of her mother. Gingerly she accepted my outstretched hand. We sat on the couch and I introduced myself.

Briefly I related the encounter with her parents. The words 'your father' had barely left my lips before she rolled her eyes and said, with her father's sharpness, 'I don't want to study at university overseas. I'm happy here.'

I had expected as much, but it came as a relief nevertheless, if only because it meant the end of my responsibilities to the Kumars, an easy way out of my hollow promises. I told Meena not to worry, that I didn't care what she wanted to do; I had come only as a promise to her father and out of my own journalistic curiosity. This she seemed to accept, and soon her air of suspicion began to thaw. I asked her questions about her life and parents.

'Did you grow up in that house?'

'Oh, god no!' she said, her nose wrinkling in disgust. The house, or so she told me, was her parents' retirement plan. Eventually they would die there and be cremated. Meena had been raised by her aunt in Calcutta. When I asked why, she said, 'So I could go to a good school.'

Looking at her now I saw her differently, not as Mr Kumar's daughter, but as his investment. So much responsibility had been placed on her shoulders: she was a prize ram, an interest-bearing account in white heels. It was obvious she was everything her parents weren't: technologically astute, ironic and very modern, as far removed from the grimy medieval world of that house in Varanasi as it was possible to be. I thought of Mr Kumar with his forms and brochures, those pathetic bundles of the *Times of India*, the broken air-conditioning unit. Here in Electronic City, among Starbucks and Armani, he was like a space traveller returned home after a thousand years to find everything changed, the lonely relic of a dead world.

Meena broke my reverie. 'You know,' she said with a smirk, 'you're not the first person to come here and find me.'

I was slightly taken aback, not by the revelation that a string of other travellers had been roped into Mr Kumar's hare-brained scheme for his children's future—although I wondered how many others had been allowed to sleep in their bed—but by the odd pleasure she seemed to take in being at the centre of the affair. Something about her patronising tone, the sly way she had insinuated that my visit was the butt of some glorious joke, seemed to suggest that not only did she revel in this ridiculous drama but had a certain contempt for my efforts and, by extension, those of her father. Poor Mr Kumar: did he have any idea how much his children resented him?

'But tell me,' I said, 'if you don't want to go to university overseas, then why don't you just tell your parents? Why not just tell your father you're happy here?'

'Oh no!' she cried, reeling back in horror. 'I could never do that.'

And with that I saw that the lies between the Kumars and their children would go on forever, ending only when their bodies would be wrapped and burned to join that rich slick of glittering ash floating down the Ganges.

Babyland

There was something ambiguous in the tone of the woman behind the counter at the petrol station. 'Everybody always asks the way to Babyland,' she said, staring over my shoulder at nothing. Of course she may simply have been musing out loud in the way you do to make someone feel at ease: 'Oh, don't worry, you're not the first person to have missed the sign. Everybody always asks the way to Babyland.' But it wasn't that. There was something in her manner, something disconcerting. A touch of irritation, certainly, as if she was always being bugged with the same stupid question, or was always hoping to be asked another, more pertinent question but never was: 'How was your daughter's graduation?' 'Did you knit that poncho yourself?' 'Can you use that extra arm for anything, or does it just hang there?' But it wasn't just outright irritation either. There was a distant, knowing air to her tone. The sort of quality you might expect of a person whose curse it is to never be believed, someone accustomed to seeing her warnings go unheeded. 'Everybody always asks the way to Babyland,' she might as well have said, 'but they never come back.'

Babyland General Hospital, to use its full title, is in a big white building just outside Cleveland, Georgia, a small town an hour and a half's drive from Atlanta. It is not, in fact, a hospital at all but a museum of sorts, devoted to one of the strangest phenomena of the 1980s: Cabbage Patch Kids. Set in a rural landscape of uncommon beauty, Babyland looked less like a hospital than a sumptuous plantation home. Why it's called Babyland and not Cabbage Patch World or something similar is a mystery. Nevertheless, 'Babyland' suited the slightly amateur, off-brand quality of the place, a quality that served to make an already unnerving experience even more so.

The staff at Babyland were all dressed as nurses. Later I learned they were supposed to be in character. Few, however, seemed to make much effort—unless their characters were supposed to be grumpy indifferent women who worked at a fake hospital for 1980s toys. 'No, you can't go upstairs,' said one at the entrance, dressed in a stiff white cap. When I ask why not she replied, "Cause it's just offices and things. You know—official Babyland stuff.'

For a Tuesday morning, Babyland seemed to be fairly busy. Oddly, there were few children among the visitors. It was mostly adult couples, a lot of female friends and mother–daughter pairs, but some men, too. Almost everyone was white and wearing a dumpy unisex uniform of khaki shorts, white sneakers and brightly coloured polo shirts tucked into straining belts. Bucking the trend was a black girl with a foot-high mohawk dyed in alternate stripes of red and green, pushing an old lady in a wheelchair. Attached to the old lady's face was an oxygen mask connected to a tank riding on a small dolly being pushed by a lanky young man wearing a hip-hop T-shirt as long as a short dress. One after the other, they weaved their way through the crowd, like members of an obscure parade who had become lost along the route.

In the foyer of Babyland was a pair of big display cabinets full of Cabbage Patch Kids. Presumably these were rare models, because labels declared some to be worth upwards of $50,000. Needless to say, this seemed an awful lot, and how a Cabbage Patch Kid could cost as much as a luxury car was unexplained. Was there a Cabbage Patch Kid Index? Did they rise and fall against the dollar or gold? I imagined a hedge-fund manager in a skyscraper some-where pulling a cigar from his mouth and barking into a phone, 'I want everything you have in Cabbage Patch Kids. Buy, buy, buy!'

Next to the cabinets was a big cabbage-shaped throne under the Babyland logo. My boyfriend Lee and I sat on it and asked a woman to take our picture. 'Is this your first time in Babyland?' she asked. We said it was. 'Y'all have a magical time,' she said, handing back our camera.

Along the walls of the foyer were signed photos of celeb-rities who had sent their best wishes to Xavier Roberts, the creator of Cabbage Patch Kids, and Babyland. Some of them were big names, including, bizarrely, George Bush, Bill Clinton, Donald Trump, Robert De Niro and, perhaps less unexpectedly, Michael Jackson. Next to him was Brooke Shields. I had a good laugh at this because Lee and I have a long-running joke that she does nothing but sign photos of herself for the walls of businesses. Honestly, I cannot remember Brooke Shields in a film since *Blue Lagoon* yet every single drycleaner, hamburger stand or pancake house in the world has a picture of her with something written on it like, 'Eddy, go easy on the starch! Love, Brooke.' Where does she find the time? Is it possible she has even been to 99 per cent of these places or does she just spend all day going through the phonebook and sending out signed pictures of herself to confused business owners?

A large photo of Xavier Roberts—a Cleveland local, as it happened—showed a full-faced man with a well-maintained beard and a cowboy hat, surrounded by Cabbage Patch Kids. His official back story said he created the 'Little People', as they were first known, when a passion for quilting with his mother led to an interest in doll-making. As my childhood hobby was collecting 1930s and 40s film memorabilia, specialising in Hedy Lamarr, I am in no position to throw stones. It is difficult, however, to think of a gayer sentence than 'My interest in doll-making grew from a passion for quilting with my mother.' I paused for a moment, revelling in an unwarranted and spiteful sense of superiority. Forgive me. It's not often I get to feel butch by comparison.

The exhibits in Babyland consisted mostly of Cabbage Patch Kids posed in various tableaus, as if in a real maternity hospital. The largest was a 'maternity ward' where you could stare through a glass wall at the newly 'born' Cabbage Patch Kids lying in realistic Perspex cribs. Several other rooms housed wooden cribs full of 'older' dolls that children could play with and, hopefully, adopt. From behind the bars of their beds, rows of little eyes met ours.

Eerily, the dolls were stood up, their chubby arms hanging over the side as if they had been about to crawl out but had frozen the moment we walked in.

Beside us a pair of young men, a couple I thought, inspected the Cabbage Patch Kids. They were grotesquely obese in a peculiarly Southern way: a pair of misshapen cones, their midriffs fanning out in hooped petticoats of flesh. Protrusions of fat, like dough squeezed in a fist, extended from unlikely places—shoulder blades, between the thighs. From certain angles it seemed as if they were slowly melting, like a Dali painting.

'I hate to say it,' said one to the other, 'but I liked the old Babyland better.' His friend nodded in agreement as they wandered off.

This exchange raised several questions. First: there had been an old Babyland? That meant someone had built not one but two. This represented a considerable investment in the maternity-hospital-and-orphanage-for-1980s toys industry. Second: these grown men had obviously not only been to the previous Babyland but had made a special trip to this one to compare the two and found the new facility lacking. Why? Was the original built before the ban on the sale of real babies in the state of Georgia? Had there been a buffet?

In one 'ward', among the dolls and props, a nurse stood rocking a cradle. She was so heavily made up, I had at first taken her for a mannequin or life-sized doll; realising she was human and moving made me start. 'I didn't see you there,' I said, laughing.

She just nodded and continued rocking the crib. 'What's your name?' she said. I told her. 'First time, Brendan?'

'At Babyland?'

She nodded again, smiling gently.

'Yes,' I said, noting a theme in the line of questioning.

I waited for her response but she didn't say anything, just stared back into the crib and continued the rocking as if drugged or hypnotised. We left the room.

In a nearby ward were half a dozen clear plastic incubation chambers with 'premature' Cabbage Patch Kids lying encased inside. A young girl cradling a doll posed for a picture beside them. As her mother took a photo, the girl with the mohawk wheeled the old lady in. The wheelchair-bound woman pulled the mask from her face. 'Beautiful,' she wheezed. With that they turned and left, the lanky boy in the hip-hop T-shirt rolling the oxygen tank behind them. To my surprise the people in the room didn't even look at them twice, just got their daughter to pose for another picture. 'That's right, honey,' said the mother. 'Now hold her gently. Remember, she's sick, honey.'

In Babyland's gift store is a large fibreglass tree surrounded by a patch of fabric cabbages. Out of these the Cabbage Patch Kids are 'born'. I knew this because I'd seen it on TV but, disappointingly, nothing seemed to be scheduled for today. When it does happen, however, it is quite a show: a doctor appears and goes through the motions of an actual birth. He listens to the pulsating cabbage with a stethoscope, administers injections and gets the crowd to yell, 'Push! Push!' This commitment to realism was impressive but also rather sinister. After all, who was this race of enslaved Cabbage Women, forced to give birth around the clock so that a gang of cruel Nurse Ratcheds might steal their children and sell them to the highest bidder? These

Cabbage Patch Kids weren't orphans at all. This was nothing but a baby farm.

There were other important ethical implications. What rights, for instance, did a Cabbage Mother have? What if she didn't want to be burdened with endless childbirth, preferring instead to pursue a career? Was there no Cabbage Patch birth control, no abortions? And what about all the Cabbage Patch Kids no one wanted at this so-called 'orphanage': the cripples, the cretins, the Cabbage Patch Crack Babies or the sulking Cabbage Patch teens, too old to be cute, who now sat around inhaling solvents and setting fire to things. Where were they?

I wondered what they were really hiding upstairs.

In the store I got in line to buy some postcards. There weren't many people but the wait was long. Voided transactions, missing prices and credit-card trouble began to test everyone's patience. When the parents of a little girl announced she would like to adopt a doll the tension was palpable. 'What would you like to call her, honey?' asked the cashier.

'Um …'

'Maybe Mary? Or Jane? Or Elizabeth?' offered the cashier.

'Remember what you told me,' said the mother. 'Remember who you said your favourite character in the Bible was?'

'Um …'

'It was Rachel, wasn't it?'

The girl shook her head.

'Yes, it was,' said the mother. 'Remember? Rachel was the daughter of Joseph and the wife of Jacob. Remember how much you liked that story?' The little girl frowned in concentration. 'It's Rachel,' said the mother to the woman behind the counter.

The cashier filled out the extensive paperwork then made the little girl swear an oath. Her mother and father looked on in rapture as she raised her right hand and vowed to forever love and care for her Cabbage Patch Kid. Everyone else crossed their arms, cleared their throats or looked at their watches as the girl tripped on every line. There are real live children in Russia you can buy with fewer formalities, and for less money.

Finally the adoption process was over and the line began to inch forward. The cashier looked harried and stressed. Wisps of hair fell in a tangle from under her nurse's cap.

'What time is the birth today?' asked a woman in front of me.

'I'm not sure, ma'am,' said the nurse as she rang up the purchases. 'It's just whenever they go into labour.'

'So when will that be?' demanded the woman.

'I can't tell you,' she said, shaking her head. 'We usually just make an announcement when they're dilating.'

Outside, the extended family of the little girl who had adopted the Cabbage Patch Kid was waiting on benches by the car park. As she appeared, one woman clapped and cheered, as if the girl had really given birth in an actual maternity hospital. Behind her the wheelchair parade went to exit but the doors closed on them, slamming the oxygen tank loudly. The boy in the hip-hop T-shirt swore under his breath and the old lady wheezed and coughed. She was obviously on her last legs, her presence raising an uncomfortable spectre of mortality among the smiling dolls.

As she breathed into her oxygen mask, I thought it possible she might even die in Babyland. I saw her body laid out in one of the cribs, behind the Perspex of the premature ward, like Lenin, or among the cabbages under the benevolent branches of the plastic tree. And why not? After all, if Cabbage Patch Kids could be born then they could also die. It was all part of the circle of life: a reminder that we might all start out as babies but all end up as cabbage feed.

And a Happy New Year

As a white man in Asia, especially South-East Asia, cheap sex seems to be everywhere. I have been propositioned in food courts, by hotel maids, hairdressers, manicurists, waiters, tour guides and taxi drivers. You never knew where it might come from next: sometimes it seemed you could walk into the supermarket and suddenly find yourself getting a blowjob in the canned-goods aisle or face down between a pair of tits at the checkout.

These offers don't just come from prostitutes. In fact, they're often from men and women who, back home, would be considered way out of your league. Finding yourself in the unfamiliar position of being the focus of everyone's sexual attention is, of course, terrific; even if you're not interested, it's great to feel like Sophia Loren for a day.

Before you convince yourself, however, that you have missed your calling as Hugh Heffner's successor at the Playboy Mansion, it is important remember that this attention is not necessarily due to any particular charisma on your part but, rather, what I like to call the 'Two-Ten Factor'.

The Two-Ten Factor is the phenomenon whereby someone who would probably rate a 'two' in the west is automatically elevated to the status of a perfect 'ten' in Asia. Obesity, bad skin, body odour, receding hairlines, live-action roleplaying: there is no barrier too great to turn western society's rejects into Asia's leading men.

From Istanbul to Tokyo, the Two-Ten Factor is omnipresent. In China, twenty-something kids whose sexual experience extends to a picture of Lara Croft and their right hand teach English for a year and suddenly find themselves fighting off mobs of latter-day imperial courtesans. In Vietnam, sleazy, has-been journalists nurse *Quiet American* fantasies while shagging half a dozen mistresses paid in skin cream and nylons. In Thailand, delicate teenage boys in pressed pants hold the hands of overweight Dutch grandfathers with comb-overs and varicose veins, their nipples sagging through the mesh in their T-shirts.

The cause of the Two-Ten Factor is a mystery. Maybe ugly western faces look handsome to Asian eyes. Perhaps mutual incomprehensibility encourages the projection of romantic fantasies. Of course sometimes they're simply being paid, or at least supported to some degree, or at least hanging around in the hope of being whisked off to Leipzig or Des Moines or Melbourne.

You could, I suppose, call this prostitution, but in many parts of Asia—where there is a huge amount of poverty, romance is still a luxury and arranged marriages are often the norm—the definition of prostitution can get hazy. Whatever the case, it is important to be aware that the relationship between the first world and third, east and west, is never more complex than in the sexual arena, and you should always tread with care.

In Indonesian, the word *kucing* means cat. It is also slang, at least in Jakarta, for a male prostitute. I know this because whenever Mikael and I would walk the streets, groups of local toughs would rise from their positions—lounging on park benches, hanging over railings at the mall—and call: '*Kucing, kucing*!'

The cry was high and mocking, aimed primarily at my friend but designed to humiliate us both. Just to drive the point home, insults were often accompanied by ironic whistles, mocking laughter and various obscene gestures designed to evoke the act of sodomy by people with clearly only a passing understanding of its mechanics. In response, Mikael would simply roll his eyes and continue styling his hair in his make-up mirror.

Despite their rudeness, the assumption that this elegant, dark-skinned boy by my side was there on my dime was not entirely unreasonable. After all, Mikael is probably the gayest straight man I know. Because he's from South-East Asia, where everyone is hairless and petite and transvestites host talk shows, he tended to get away with it. Yet even by the elastic standards of Asian masculinity, Mikael made Freddie Mercury look like John Wayne.

Mikael's adventures in fashion were legendary. For a period while we were at university he took to carrying a handbag—not a manbag, an actual handbag—which he would hold waist-high in front of him, as though pouring tea, as he shuffled around campus in closed-toed sandals. During another bold journey into androgyny he started wearing his girlfriend's underpants, the elastic waist pulled high above low-slung jeans to reveal rows of little satin bows and lace trim. When I said he looked ridiculous he replied in an aggrieved tone, 'But this is what Dior is doing this season!'

As if his reputation needed any help, almost all of Mikael's friends were gay, none more so than Dao. Short and very slight, Dao was a tiny camp whirlwind, a fast-forward kabuki of flapping wrists, clanking bangles and cackling laughter. Dao was a wedding planner, giving him access to a broad range of accessories he often styled in innovative ways: the night I met him he wore a lace petticoat fashioned into a shawl.

'I like this one,' he said, giving a little twirl. 'I want my wife to wear it when we get married.'

'Your wife?'

'Yes,' said Dao, adjusting the volume of lace about his throat. 'I'm going to marry my third cousin. It's all arranged. I don't want to get married, but I'll do it for Mama.' From his wallet he produced a photo of himself in a tuxedo together with a young woman in an elaborate wedding gown. 'This is the pre-wedding wedding photo. It's important to get all the details right. I have seen so many styling disasters.'

'Does your mother know you're gay?' I asked.

Dao cocked an eyebrow and gave a sharp little laugh. Spreading his shawl out he looked at me and said, 'Does she *know* I'm gay?'

An excellent guide to Jakarta, Dao knew every sleazy bar, pirate DVD store or restaurant serving soups of the genitals of endangered species. One night he took us to a gay nightclub hidden in the back of a mall. It had been quite a feat to find because it was Ramadan and many bars were closed. Those that remained open did so discreetly; an

MC reminded us to leave quietly: rogue Islamists were currently driving around Jakarta in minivans, invading nightclubs with machetes. The previous week they had attacked a famous club not far away and slashed the legs of women in short skirts.

For a time we sat and watched a hilarious drag show, made all the more scandalous for taking place in the Islamic holy month. On stage two wild-eyed queens performed a mother-and-daughter prostitute routine in Indonesian.

'What's this?' demanded the mother, making an accusatory gesture at the daughter, nose deep in a book. 'You're reading the Koran, you slut!'

'It's okay,' replied the daughter. 'I just took nine ecstasy tablets.'

The audience roared.

'And you're wearing a headscarf now?' said the mother, flicking at the covering on her head. 'You think you're holy or something? Who do you think you're fooling?'

'It's okay,' said the daughter, rubbing her rubber breasts. 'I'm not wearing any underwear.'

Anyone who says that they don't enjoy to some degree the privileges that come with being a white man in much of Asia is probably lying. To be western in Asia is to be ushered backstage into an alien world of entitlement and gratification: waiters become extra obsequious, security guards ignore you at checkpoints and you can wear nothing but a beach towel and bouncers will still treat you like Andy Warhol arriving at Studio 54. With prices generally quite low, life is full of little treats normally out of your reach. You can dine in fine restaurants, have clothes made and need never do your own laundry again. Every morning in Jakarta I drank a smoothie made of four mangoes cut before my eyes. I still dream of those bowel movements.

Of all the extravagant pleasures of the Orient there are few I indulge in more than massages. Whether being pummelled by a blind woman in Cambodia or a lady boy on a beach in Thailand, I cannot think of anything $5 can buy that will bring you more happiness. So when we left the bar early and Dao suggested we all get massages, I agreed enthusiastically.

'I know the place,' said Dao. 'Not very far. I think you like it very maarsh!'

As we walked it quickly became apparent that Dao was taking us to one of Jakarta's largest gay brothels. I admit I had been (sort of) expecting this: entirely 'legitimate' massage services in South-East Asia are almost nonexistent and most double as whorehouses, as do a number of other businesses, notably karaoke bars and beauty parlours. In Jakarta there are even 'furniture salesmen' who will come to your house with catalogues of chairs and tables and photos of the girls or boys they represent discreetly tucked in the middle. Nevertheless, I was slightly anxious.

I had recently moved in with my boyfriend, the first time I had made such a commitment. Call me old-fashioned, but I didn't feel we were yet at the Indonesian-rent-boy-in-sleazy-Jakarta-brothel stage of our relationship, and I didn't want to rush things.

'Okay, Dao,' I said. 'But do you promise me that we can just get a massage without sex?'

'Oh yeah, yeah, yeah,' said Dao. 'It's no problem. Trust me!' With a flick of his shawl he bustled down the busy Jakarta street, a blur of white lace in the night.

I chose Rico because he seemed the least predatory. As we walked in, a dozen or so boys immediately turned their attention from the television and stared, each adopting his best come-hither look, eyes painting us up and down. 'Which one you like?' asked the madam, an ageing Chinese rent boy with a lucky moonstone ring like a small eyeball on his pinkie finger. I looked at the field of boys: clad in white linen wraparound vests and matching culottes with thigh-high slits they looked like devotees of a cult dedicated to the worship of Ziggy Stardust. Gently licking their lips or running fingers coquettishly through their hair, they lounged on couches or cushions spread across the cool marble floor. It was like choosing a lobster from a tank if the lobster could rape you.

'Um … I think he'll be fine,' I said, pointing to the only one still watching the soap opera.

The madam summoned Rico. He walked over and shook my hand in a gesture of unexpected western formality. Dao, meanwhile, skipped off down the corridor hand in hand with some muscular kick-boxer type. With the closing of their door, a few muffled shrieks echoed down the corridor.

I leaned over to the madam. 'I just want to make sure he knows: no sex, okay? Just a massage. That's alright, yes?'

'Oh yes,' said the madam. 'Don't worry, no problem. It's all arranged.' He waved his hand and the moonstone gave a pearly flash in the fluorescent light.

———

In the room it was dark except for a dim golden nightlight in the corner. Rico left me to undress and I lay on the table in my towel. Soon he reappeared and began to smear my back with scented oil. He was shirtless, which made me a little apprehensive. I tried to make light conversation. 'Where are you from, Rico?'

'From Sulawesi,' he said, rubbing my shoulders. 'I am Christian.'

'Uh-huh. And how long have you lived in Jakarta?'

'Six months.'

'Why did you come here?'

'Because I like to live in Jakarta.'

'Hm.'

Rico moved further down my back. 'I love white skin,' he said, sliding down my spine to the waist. 'Your skin is so beautiful.' He paused. 'You are beautiful.'

'Thank you, Rico,' I said, aware that while compliments on one's skin were, perhaps, not part of the masseur's professional code, he was, at least, doing a good job.

Gradually, Rico worked his way further down. Loosening my towel he lowered it to expose my backside. 'When I am in Sulawesi, we sing beautiful song in church,' he said softly in my ear. 'I am very good singer.' Gently he began to rub the mounds of my buttocks. 'Were you there when they crucified my Lord?' he sang, kneading up and down. 'Were you there when they crucified, my Lord? Oh, sometime, it causes me to tremble, *tremble*. Were you there when they crucified, my Lord?'

I couldn't deny it: he was a good singer. He was also slightly overstepping the boundaries of what I regarded as a purely platonic massage. Slowly his hands moved lower and lower, deeper into the crevice of my backside.

'Rico?'

'Yes?' he said, leaning down into my ear and breathing softly.

'No sex, okay? Just massage?'

'Oh yes,' he said, yanking the towel away and exposing me completely. 'Just massage.'

Rico began to run his hands across the tops of my thighs. 'At Christmas we sing the best songs. You know "Away in a Manger"?' The question was rhetorical. He began again. 'Away in a manger, no crib for a bed ...' As he sang, his strokes became more forceful, his thumbs dipping between my thighs, each upstroke brushing my scrotum. 'The little Lord Jesus lay down his sweet head.'

I was not yet 100 per cent sure, but I was fairly certain that my naive desire for a non-sexual massage at the male brothel had been thwarted. I allowed Rico a few more strokes then cleared my throat loudly. 'Ah, excuse me, Rico. But I think I might stop now.'

His fingers continued their explorations of my perineum.

'Ah, Rico?'

'Yes?' he said, gently fondling my left testicle.

'We're finished now.'

'Finish you?'

'No. Finish. Over. I have to go.'

Rico's tone became alarmed. 'Why? Why you have to go?' He began madly sliding his hands up and down my body. 'It's okay,' he said, pressing his muscular chest against my back as he leaned into my ear. 'I am Christian.'

'Thanks. I know, Rico.'

Frantically he began to knead my backside. 'But I have Dutch boyfriend!' he exclaimed, as if somehow that might cinch the deal. Once more he burst into song, his voice containing a hint of desperation: 'Silent night, holy night. Shepherds quake, at the sight …' His hands ran down my legs and back between my buttocks. 'Round yon Virgin, mother and child …' His middle finger began to gently nuzzle into my sphincter.

I sat up. Rico's face was confused, almost frantic. Squatting down he grabbed me by the thighs and looked up, past my semi-aroused penis and into my eyes. He began to sing. 'We wish you a merry Christmas, we wish you a merry Christmas.' His tone was sultry and husky, nightclubby and beseeching. 'And a happy New Year.' He lay his head on my thigh and began to move his open mouth towards my crotch.

I grabbed the towel and retreated to the other side of the room. 'I think I'll just have a shower now, Rico.'

'But it's okay,' he said, gesturing to the table, begging me to reconsider. 'I have Dutch boyfriend! I am Christian!'

All at once I realised what was happening: Rico thought he had done a bad job, that my reluctance—which he had initially read as a face-saving tactic I'd adopted out of some fear of being identified as 'gay'—was actually due to something he had done wrong. I could see the panicked scenarios going through his head: I would complain; he'd be kicked out of the brothel and end up in a slum or having to return to his village in Sulawesi where he'd be forced to go back to singing with his mother in the choir and blowing the banana seller at the bus stop.

Here was the dark flipside of the Two-Ten Factor: as much as being a celebrity was fantastic, the power that came with it was a burden. Being able to ruin the lives of boys like Rico was not my idea of a good time. As much fun as it was to be Superman, I was happier as Clark Kent.

I knew only one way out of this. Grabbing my wallet I pulled out the money and dumped it on the bed: 7000 rupiah. I couldn't work out how much it was in dollars but was fairly sure it would be enough of a tip. Besides, it was all I had on me. 'For you, Rico,' I said. 'Thanks very much.' It was the same tone you might have used to thank a plumber: *Good work on the kitchen pipes, Larry. Here's a little something for the hand job*. But the chummy tone only seemed to make the situation more awkward.

Rico looked at the money like it was a dead rat. As I retreated into the bathroom his eyes followed me, full of hurt. Closing the door, I listened to his last pitiable attempts to draw me out. 'We wish you a Merry Christmas,' he sang, his voice beginning to crack. 'We wish you a Merry Christmas. And a happy New Year.'

I turned on the shower and when I came out he and the money were gone.

In the foyer the boys were all still spread about on their cushions, watching a new TV show. Mikael sat on an armchair among them holding a cup of instant coffee. Rico was nowhere to be seen. 'You didn't go in?' I asked.

'No, of course not.'

'Why?'

'Because it's a gay brothel.'

'But I thought we were all getting massages?'

'Not me. People only come here for sex.'

'I didn't.'

'Oh, I just thought you were lying because you were embarrassed.'

A little while later Dao appeared, freshly showered and looking very pleased with himself. 'Oh, that was great,' he said, dropping into an armchair and adjusting his lace throw. 'He asked me to rim him. His arse was really nice, so—how you say?—*fragrant*. He say to me, "Oh you're really good at that." And he is fucking guys all day, so this is a real compliment.'

The madam joined us and began chatting with Dao in Indonesian. The two cackled and slapped one another like old friends. 'And Rico,' said the madam, turning to me. 'He was good?'

'Yes, fine,' I said. 'Where did he go?'

'Just to get something to eat,' he said and scratched at the corner of his mouth with the moonstoned pinkie. Turning to Dao, he said something in Indonesian that made him and Mikael laugh so loudly all the boys turned to stare.

I asked Dao what he had said. The madam made a hasty exit. Dao gave a shriek: 'He said, "But I don't think he can eat very much for only 7000 rupiah."' He and Mikael laughed again, slapping their thighs and rocking back in their chairs. The boys in their Ziggy Stardust outfits went back to their TV show. Apparently 7000 rupiah was about fifty cents. Rico probably thought it was just my way of rubbing salt in the wounds.

Of course, part of me felt he should have been happy with anything: what was the going rate for being sexually assaulted, anyway? Ten per cent? Fifteen? Victim's discretion? Mostly I just wanted to clear the air, wanted to tell Rico it wasn't him or me, it was money and power and sex that got in the way; in another time, another place, we might have been friends and equals.

Now I imagined him walking the streets of Jakarta, cursing my memory and wishing me an eternity of unhappy Christmases. That hurt a little, but as I would never see him again I guessed I'd just have to wear it: if there's something I've learned, it's that not every story can have a happy ending.

Stays in Vegas

I had only spent one night in Las Vegas prior to buying a home there, and didn't even have a very good time. Until moving to Las Vegas the city existed in my memory only as a series of strange, somewhat desolate images: a floor of slot machines stretching into infinity, the ching-ching-ching of a million payouts reverberating through my body like the high-frequency chirping of a billion jungle insects; a compulsive eater gobbling down a clock face of pink desserts, waterfalls of flesh spilling over his chair; ending up, somehow, at an after-party for the DJ Moby, watching a group of models fuss over the bald man at their centre, half their size and uncomfortable with the attention.

Considering my experience of Las Vegas, my decision more than ten years later to buy a home there might seem slightly strange. Arguably stranger still: buying it online, sight unseen, after drinking a bottle of red wine and with only the assurances of a man claiming to be a Las Vegas real estate agent called 'Uncle Jack' who might as well have been a Ukranian mafioso sitting in a room in Kiev for all I knew. I can't buy a pair of theatre tickets online with confidence; how I managed to make the biggest financial transaction of my life as casually as I might download a song is still something I can't quite fathom. Looking back, it was as if I had been in the possession of some stronger, altogether more confident being with the power of foresight and the knowledge that I could not allow my neurotic indecisiveness to blow it again.

Why move to Las Vegas? The short answer is because it was cheap. The long answer crosses continents and is so difficult to articulate as to be really nothing more than the subconscious whim of instinct.

Around the age of thirty I came into a relatively small, unforeseen lump of cash which, of course, I immediately started spending on travel, alcohol and the kind of junk that winds up on eBay in six months. I decided I needed to invest before the money completely disappeared.

For some time I had been toying with the idea of buying a home overseas, perhaps with an eye to living there permanently. Although I'd spent a great deal of time travelling, often for extended periods, I had never really settled anywhere. It wasn't that I didn't like Australia, but aspects of it had begun to get on my nerves: its smallness, its petty paternalism, the fact that all my friends, apparently in some kind of coordinated pre-planned strike, had given birth and now seemed to be under the misapprehension that I enjoyed sitting in parks, feeding ducks and discussing school waiting lists as much as they did.

I started looking into getting a home overseas, somewhere cheap. Asia was a possibility: balmy and exotic with a steady supply of poor people to make my bed and cook me snacks. Unfortunately it was a red-tape nightmare and not really that cheap.

One day, while on assignment in Beijing, I met an artist who was to become my friend. A few months later, over dinner in Australia, I discovered he had lived in the States for five years. I explained my predicament. 'Why not Las Vegas?' he said.

Why not Las Vegas? You might as well ask why I don't sleep on a bed of nails or take a beach holiday in eastern Japan. On paper, Las Vegas had little to recommend it. The city had been terribly affected by the American sub-prime crisis, worse even than Detroit. Most homes were worth less than their owners had paid and unemployment was way above the national average. Plus, Las Vegas wasn't a real place—was it?—just a giant theme park in the desert. Apart from—I dunno—Celine Dion, some gay German magicians and every hopeless alcoholic drifter on the west coast, who actually lived there? Did it even have normal things like schools, Walmart and local news bulletins with stories about college football and an awkward live cross to a wacky weatherman in a park where the Rotary Club was frying the world's biggest pancake?

The idea of moving to Vegas was absurd. And yet, occasionally, something gets stuck in your mind, an uncomfortable grain of sand turning slowly to a pearl, and soon I came round to the idea.

Vegas was cheap. Insanely, dubiously cheap. Sydney had become more expensive than New York City; the money I had couldn't have bought me a parking space. The idea that I could buy a three-bedroom home in the entertainment capital of America for $60,000 seemed absurd. That it might be designed by a prominent mid-modern architect in the suburb in which Martin Scorsese filmed *Casino* and where Dean Martin, Phyllis Diller and Debbie Reynolds had once lived seemed like some cruel hoax. *What's the catch?* I wondered.

Well, some might say the catch was I had to live in Las Vegas. Yet the more I researched the city the more I liked it. It had a great climate, some of the world's best restaurants, was connected by air to just about every city in the world, and every night there was a performance by a band, comedian or forgotten cabaret singer I had longed to see my whole life. Plus, it was Vegas. Storied city of song and dance, home of Howard Hughes, the mafia, Frank Sinatra and fat Elvis. Of course, it was also the home of addictive personalities, gun crime and, according to *Las Vegas Jailhouse*, hookers with meth face and their volatile boyfriends strapped into Hannibal Lecter chairs designed to stop them spitting at people.

Whether these associations were anything more than the usual flashcard clichés didn't really matter. It was more important to discover whether the near-unconscious compulsion that had led me to buy a house in the first place had been a good one. Could Las Vegas really be my new home? Whatever the outcome, I couldn't prevaricate forever. Like so many before me, I decided to book a ticket, get on a plane and take a gamble on Las Vegas.

Straight off the plane I drive to my new house where I meet Uncle Jack, who is, to my relief, real and waiting for me. The house is everything I'd hoped and more, full of gorgeous mid-modern touches: butterfly roof, mirrored wall in the living room, a period 'floating' fireplace made of a single piece of cast iron. Unfortunately, it has also been empty a long time and the windows don't lock. A broken glass tube and some burnt paper are evidence that someone has been smoking drugs in the living room. They haven't done anything else—there's no vandalism or unflushed turds in the toilet—but it's not very reassuring.

The next day I go and buy some locks. It is night by the time I get to the house. The electricity has yet to be turned on and I can hardly see anything. Suddenly, I hear a noise. 'Hello? Is anybody there?' Silence. My mind begins to race. I have seen those shows about people in America who have fought off lunatics; I know what happens next. A psychotic crackhead is in the house. He is waiting for me, readying himself for an attack.

'If there's anybody here, you'd better leave now.'

As my words echo I am struck by the incongruity of my voice. My accent is not strong. A lot of Americans don't even realise I'm Australian; many assume I'm English, and for quite a few of those I might as well be Prince William. A crackhead was likely to be puzzled or amused but unlikely to feel intimidated. He might have been more afraid had I threatened to slap him with a glove.

I decide to adopt an American accent. For reasons unknown, it is Southern, or at least my idea of a Southern accent. 'Yo! Y'all better get outta here before the police come,' I yell, pronouncing 'police' in two separate syllables—*po-lease*—like I'm Dolly Parton or Daisy Duke. 'I'm givin' y'all a chance. Yo! Anybody in here? Anybody?'

Silence. For a while I stand in the dark, feeling stupid and afraid. For the first time since I had the idea of moving to Las Vegas I begin to entertain the possibility that I have done a very hasty, very foolish thing.

———

No one tells you that the landscape around Las Vegas is beautiful. The intense light and brilliant colours make everything sharply defined, hyper-real. Everyday scenes are made weird and weird scenes, of which there are many, become almost hallucinatory. Some days, driving the uncluttered freeways, Las Vegas seems almost dreamlike, as if you have slipped momentarily into an altered present, a world both familiar and strange, a civilisation rebuilt after a forgotten apocalypse.

On the freeway I drive past a man walking on the shoulder against the traffic. He is wearing nothing but a pair of jeans and a series of circular electrodes attached to his chest, wires dangling from them. I guess he has escaped from a hospital but he looks like a fleeing captive from a secret sci-fi experiment. Where is he going? What will he tell people when he arrives? In this town, I am soon to learn, it's unlikely anyone will notice.

———

Seeing Las Vegas from the air for the first time, I am immediately struck by its physical isolation, the crisp definition of its borders in the desert. Like a fried egg dropped on a big red carpet it oozes out then simply stops. Unlike most other major American urban areas there's no debate about where Vegas begins and ends, no commuter towns, satellite cities or suburbs being sucked into its orbit. Las Vegas stops where the desert starts.

One day my boyfriend Lee and I decide to drive between the city's two furthest points. Many of the housing developments on the fringes were abandoned after the recession. A lot seem only half-inhabited, if that. Many have taped-up windows and no trespassing signs. We see almost no one.

Standing at the last row of homes is a very strange sensation. On one side it's suburban America: the 'adobe' houses rendered in Styrofoam, each so like its neighbour it's as if one building were being infinitely reflected in a pair of facing mirrors. Then, as you look the other way, the illusion is shattered: all you see is miles of empty brown earth and barren hills rising into red mountains. It's like one of those dreams where you discover a hidden door that takes you to some faraway land.

Standing at the edge of Vegas is a reminder that this city is built in the middle of a place not strictly meant for human habitation. In fact, outside the Persian Gulf there isn't a city on this scale in such a hostile environment. Nothing grows in Las Vegas, there's no water and walking anywhere can literally kill you. How is it possible that the barrier between this deadly desert and civilisation can be nothing but a row of little backyards filled with faded play equipment? Who decided it would end here? It seems so arbitrary, so flimsy, almost an imaginary border: like a kid drawing a chalk line across 'their' half of the pavement and demanding that the remorseless amoral power of Mother Nature stay on *its* side of the mock-adobe garden wall.

On our way home we drive past our local mall to see the fire department extinguishing a flaming palm tree. It must be at least 25 metres tall and when the water hits the trunk it turns black and runs a charcoal river across the road. I suppose someone must have lit it, though for what reason I can't imagine. Perhaps it just spontaneously combusted in the heat.

———

The next day I apply to have our electricity turned on. The office is in the middle of a very sketchy North Las Vegas neighbourhood. The wait is more than an hour. Children are crying and everyone is yelling into their phones in Spanish. A guy behind me is arguing with the guard. His girlfriend looks on passively, a baby on her hip.

I finally put in my application and wait outside on the step for my ride. Suddenly, the argumentative guy comes charging out, swinging the door so hard it hits the glass wall, causing it to wobble. He is making gang signs and chanting, 'Money, power, respect. Money, power, respect.' As they make their way to their car, his girlfriend interrupts him. 'Why'd yo have to get all up in her face, So Real?'

'Fuckin' bitch,' says So Real. 'Givin' me attitude. Bitch lucky I didn't fuckin' kill da bitch.' The girl sighs heavily. 'I love you, So Real.'

———

Las Vegas seems to be the exception to every rule: the small big city; the Mormon town where everything is legal; a place where polygamists and apocalypse nuts waiting in their compounds for the coming One World Government live comparatively peacefully alongside celebrity impersonators and a slew of French Canadian acrobats of exceptional fruitiness.

How to classify Las Vegas? What other cities can you say it is like? Dubai? Macau? Neither, really. Each share some of the superficial trappings of Vegas but none of its anarchic intensity. Where does it fit within the United States? It's nominally part of the south-west, but it couldn't really be classified as south-western. There's none of that corn-on-pizza and kachina doll crap you get in Arizona or New Mexico; none of those wan-looking women with long grey hair and turquoise jewellery selling Indian blankets and patchwork leather goods, thank god.

It's sort of 'west coast', but looking at the landscape between Vegas and LA, the warm waters of the Pacific may as well be on Mars rather than a four-hour drive away. Besides, historically and culturally, despite its libertine reputation, Vegas has as much, if not a great deal more, in common with Mormon Utah than the carefree sensuality of California. But you need only to drive to Salt Lake City, starched and pressed and smelling of cookies and soap, to see that Vegas is totally unlike its slightly younger, *much* sluttier sister: if they were people, Salt Lake City would be lucky to see Vegas once a year at Thanksgiving between child access visits, random drug tests from her parole officer and crystal meth hits in the bathroom.

We try to get to know some of our neighbours. I manage to have a conversation with most, even the schizophrenic hoarder next door who steals our garbage at night. The only ones I don't meet are the black family who live in a rundown house opposite. I can't figure out who actually lives there; people are always coming and going and there's often a drama. One day, while they are out, two of their three pit bulls attack and almost kill the third. For hours it lies whimpering against the fence, covered in blood, while we try to fend off the murderous pair with sticks.

A guy who drives a beaten-up Cadillac seems to have a particularly volatile relationship with everyone else in the house. One day he comes out the front door screaming, then drives across the yard, sending garbage bins flying, as well as a lawn chair and bunch of lumber that has sat there for a while for no ostensible reason. After the car has disappeared around the corner, a little girl comes out of the house and builds a teepee from the lumber. For a while she hangs out inside, talking to herself and having an imaginary tea party in the dirt.

———

America is full of people who think they're eccentric because they have taken up a wacky hobby designed to draw attention to themselves. These people are a plague in towns like Austin, Portland or anywhere with craft beers and no black people. 'Oh, you should meet Annie. She's hilarious. She knits dolls of Abraham Lincoln, only eats white food and sends postcards to people who have the same name as her.' Or, 'I think you'd really like my friend Dave. Dave is a gas. He dresses like Jimmy Cagney in *Public Enemy*, refuses to listen to music recorded after

1939 and is really rude to everybody. He's a real character. Totally eccentric.'

These people are not eccentrics. Mostly they're just arse-holes. A true eccentric is never self-conscious: they are a universe to themselves and have no idea they are considered strange. They couldn't be any different if they tried. By this measure, Las Vegas seems to have more genuinely eccentric people than any other place I've been in America. Why? Probably because there's no audience in Las Vegas for people who are trying to be 'characters': you have got to be pretty fucking crazy before anyone pays you much attention in this town. In Vegas, kooky hobbies and outfits just aren't going to cut it. This is the crazy big league.

It's Halloween. We've been invited to a party so go shopping for costumes. The store is huge and playing 'creepy' music to get everyone in the spirit. Now and then there is a scream so loud it must be real. I am slightly disturbed but dismiss it as part of the ambience and keep browsing. Turning a corner I see a tall thin man standing in an aisle with a two-foot macaw on his shoulder. I assume he must be doing a promotion but quickly realise he is simply browsing for a Halloween costume. He smiles at us, revealing one—and I mean *one*—tooth. The macaw screams again and shits down his back. All I can think is: *Sir, you have one tooth and a macaw on your shoulder. Why do you need a costume when every day is Halloween?*

Vegas is a city of unexpected convergences, haphazard assemblies. Constantly you see little groups and wonder, *How the hell did these people find one another?* How did that teenage Chinese boy end up hanging out with that obese mid-forties black woman in silver hot pants and that white body builder in his early twenties with a glam-rock haircut and a tank top that reads *Hard Rock Café Villeneuve*?

Walking down Fremont Street I see a couple. He is black and, I guess, in his fifties. She is white and in her late forties. He has a flattop, is wearing a white velour tracksuit embroidered with gold detailing, a pair of white brogues and ropes of gold chains that hang as low as his navel and make a jangling sound when he walks. She is wearing a long-sleeved, ankle-length prairie dress, a pair of Estelle Getty glasses and has her hair piled in a loose, billowing bun. He looks like Flavor Flav as captain of the Love Boat. She looks like she just escaped a cult. They are holding hands and, sometimes, kissing.

Like a hidden army of fat Daleks ready to rise up and kill us all at the command of their leader, people in electric wheelchairs are everywhere in Las Vegas. You see them playing the slots, moving their way along buffet lines, even in burger chain drive-throughs. The vast majority are not disabled, just too fat to walk. A billboard for a company that sells the chairs appeals directly to this market. Tired of walking? it asks, as if walking were a pesky bodily function rendered unnecessary by technology.

It is tempting to apply the same logic to everything. Tired of breathing? Tired of eating? Tired of wearing clothes?

I envision a future Las Vegas in which everyone rolls down the street, naked, hooked up to feeding tubes and respirators. Some days that vision doesn't seem particularly far-fetched.

———

There are a few electric-wheelchair people in our area who have become familiar figures. One man often spotted at the El Cortez, an old Downtown casino, has modified his so he can lie completely flat, as if he were on a li-lo floating around a swimming pool. I assume he used to be some sort of naval officer because he always wears a captain's hat and a blue blazer with gold buttons. Of course, my assumption may be wrong. It is just as likely he has never seen the ocean.

Also near us is a guy who we sometimes see driving against the traffic on one of the city's busiest streets. Cars honk and screech around him as he travels but he pays them no attention. On his lap he always carries a shiny alto saxophone. Where is he going? The road he's on is huge and miles from anywhere you could play a saxophone and hope to be heard. Yet there he is: always on his way to some concert somewhere far, far away. Somewhere that exists, perhaps, only in his mind.

———

There are a lot of drifters and crooks in Vegas. I guess that's not exactly news to anyone, but the number and sheer shadiness of the junkies, homeless and assorted shifty characters is pretty extreme, even by the standards of a big city.

One day I discover the online Sex Offender Registry and am immediately fascinated. A map marked with red dots indicates the addresses of any registered offenders in the area. A block of very rundown apartments a short walk from my place has so many it looks like our neighbourhood has chickenpox.

I spend hours filing through the photos and profiles. They tell you everything: hair and eye colour, known aliases, tattoos, even scars and missing fingers.

The tattoos are particularly fascinating. One guy has dozens of bears all over his body. Another, convicted of Lewdness with a Child (Attempt), has something called a 'clown collage' on his upper left arm. One who did time for Statutory Sexual Seduction—which sounds, to my mind, like the title of a Barry White album—has a 'woman shooting aliens' on his chest. A particularly nasty character with a long string of violent offences has this description: 'Back: *Motherfuck You.*'

The crimes range from the comparatively minor to lengthy checklists of brutal transgressions. Until reading the Sex Offender Registry I didn't know there was such a thing as Forcible Oral Sodomy. One guy that really terrifies me has his convictions listed as: 'Rape/Force/Fear/etc.'. *Etcetera?* What the hell does *etcetera* mean? I mean: I can imagine a lot of sick shit. Are there things I'm just supposed to assume go with rape, force and fear?

One very hot day we are in a restaurant called Pepe's Tacos. In the distance, through the heat haze, I see a figure crossing Boulder Highway. I am unsure if it is male or female but the marionette gait is of a universal and immediately recognisable type known as 'junkie walk'.

As the figure draws near I see it is a woman. Arriving at the restaurant, she flings open the door and approaches the drink machine. She is holding a filthy jumbo-sized paper cup, seemingly fished out of the garbage. 'Don't mind me,' she calls to the manager behind the counter. 'I just want some water.' She puts her cup beneath the Sprite tap and fills it. A girl mopping the floor looks at her boss, unsure of what to do. The manager rolls her eyes, and goes back to taking orders.

The junkie makes herself at home. She is completely high, but affable. Leaning against the counter, she drinks her Sprite and addresses the girl mopping the floor.

'You got a hard job, honey.'

The girl smiles weakly.

The junkie gulps down her drink and fills up another. 'You bilingual?' she asks.

'Huh?' says the girl.

'Bilingual, you know: bi, meaning "two", "lingual", language. You speak two languages?'

The girl's brow creases in confusion. She stops mopping.

'You speak Spanish?' says the junkie, exasperated that her brief lesson in etymology has fallen on such barren ground.

'Of course,' says the girl.

'You gotta be bilingual to do this job?'

'Yeah, to take the orders.'

The junkie shakes her head slowly and sighs in a way that seems to indicate the unfairness of the world. It is not a specific sigh, she is not resentful of anyone's success or bitter about her own failures; her pain is existential.

'I'm not bilingual,' announces the junkie. 'You need to be bilingual in this town to get a job and that's the truth. They say French is the hardest language you can learn.' She downs the rest of her drink then refills her cup with more Sprite. 'But I don't speak French. Too hard. Anyway,' she says, flinging open the back door and addressing the entire restaurant, 'what do I need a job for?' She raises her Sprite as though toasting us. 'I already got a fuckin' job,' she shouts. 'It's called being me!'

And with that she makes her exit, the door slamming, her thin figure disappearing into the hot Vegas streets where, I like to think, she may walk still, just being her.

Until I arrived in Las Vegas it hadn't really occurred to me that the reason I was getting my house cheap was because someone else had lost it. When Uncle Jack tells me the people who had owned it previously were relatively well-off investors it makes me feel a little better, but doesn't really negate the principle nor change the fact they might have as easily been a family of six who are now living under a bridge.

My neighbourhood is mostly Latino and unemployment is high; I realise I have underestimated how poor it is. To make ends meet some people drive around selling snacks, drinks and newspapers out of their cars, honking their horns as they approach. One woman doesn't have a car so she rings a bicycle bell and pushes a shopping cart she has taken from a local supermarket. In it is a box full of tamales. She sells the tamales for $3. One evening I buy one. Her English is not good but she tells me she has three children and some evenings sells four or five tamales.

At first I worry our neighbours will hate us. Talking with them I realise many have lost their homes. I try to imagine how they might see us: *Hi there, we're the rich Australian gays who had nothing better to do with our pots of money than swan into your decaying neighbourhood and buy your home out from underneath you. Don't mind us. Please, feel free to go about desperate subsistence lives. We'll just sit back here and enjoy a few cocktails while you clip coupons and cook your cat.*

To my surprise, however, they all seem quite friendly. In fact, a number congratulate me on my (entirely imaginary) business smarts. The thought occurs to me that, perhaps, they are just being nice while secretly plotting to sneak in one night while I'm asleep and drive a stake through my head. But it doesn't seem that way. Perhaps the American belief in the inherent goodness of entrepreneurship and the accumulation of wealth trumps all else? Whatever the case, the poverty of Las Vegas often takes me aback. I am still shocked by scenes many Americans seem to think are normal: crowds of Mexican men in front of Home Depot offering labour for the price of gum; churchy black ladies standing on street corners collecting for a child's funeral. When I meet someone who tells me he works in a warehouse for $10 an hour I am about to say, 'Oh, that's awful,' because in Australia kids in juice bars can make twice that, until he says, 'Which is obviously really good.'

Hm, yes. Obviously.

Every day in our neighbourhood we get people knocking on our door asking to do various jobs: tree trimming, house painting, concreting. A number of these I hire out of sheer guilt. After years of trying to harden my heart against moist-eyed beggar children and all the rest I thought I'd be immune by now. But it's no good: they still get me, every time.

A woman quotes us fifty bucks for five hours of house cleaning. This seems a ridiculously good deal, but we soon discover it's a false economy—she moves at a pace more usually associated with wind erosion on stone. Watching her dust I am reminded of a tree sloth or a performance of Japanese Noh theatre. As she opens a bottle of bleach at quarter speed I wonder if it's possible she is an alien still keeping the time of her distant, slowly rotating planet: seconds are half an hour, hours are months. She is probably 9000 Earth years old.

Between us we start referring to her as Señora SloMo. I try all sorts of techniques to speed her up: bustling busily about the house, hoping to inspire her; putting on high-tempo music; talking on the phone and saying 'immigration' loudly every few seconds. Nothing works. Señora SloMo will not be hurried. She is an unchanging constant, a transcendent being, indifferent to the petty phenomena of the physical world.

Another door-to-door hire is Alejandro, who arrives one day on a bicycle. He and his brother paint the entire outside of the house for $500. Or, rather, his brother paints while Alejandro watches and eats a burrito.

At first I like Alejandro. In spite of his poor English he is good-humoured and talkative. He answers all my questions with one word: 'eh-zack-a-lee'. He always says it in a tone that is conspiratorial, rich in implication, as though we are Renaissance courtiers and I had just obliquely suggested we poison the Pope and install our political puppet. A sly little smile, a raised eyebrow, an intense gaze: 'Ah, yes. Eh-zack-a-lee.'

Soon, however, I decide Alejandro is a lazy pain in the neck who can't be trusted. His brother, who doesn't speak any English, does everything except paint the doors. These Alejandro eventually does at my insistence, resentfully slopping on an uneven coat while they are closed. Once he has left I pry them open and redo them all.

When they finish for the day, Alejandro takes the money. I notice he only gives his brother $200. I suspect he has lied to him. 'Alejandro,' I say, 'your brother knows it's $500, right?'

Alejandro looks at me with a little smile and a raised eyebrow. 'Ah, yes. Eh-zack-a-lee.'

There are two lives you can live in America: with a car and without. Vegas might be the worst city in America to be in the latter category. With its heat, freeways and strip malls, this city is especially unkind to pedestrians. Everywhere you look in Vegas someone is trekking miles across a wasteland of shoe-melting asphalt, juggling their groceries while trying to stop their kid getting pancaked by an SUV. Nine times out of ten they look exactly the same: Latin, female and very tired.

The bus stops in Vegas are like a nature-documentary scene of a single tree in the middle of a baking plane under which 5 million caribou are competing for a bit of shade. All day people sit by the roadside, wilting in the heat, waiting for buses that never seem to come to take them on journeys that never seem to end among a crowd that never seems to shut up.

We are on the bus in early summer. Temperatures are approaching record highs and building. In front of us, two girls are discussing their attempts to stay cool. One mentions her air conditioning needs repairing.

'This motherfucker sweat a *lot*,' replies her friend, referring to herself in the third person as 'this motherfucker'. 'Gotta wash the sheets every other motherfuckin' day. This motherfucker be *sweatin'* at night. This motherfucker don't have air. Just be sittin' on the sofa and be *sweatin'*! This motherfucker take a cool shower, because that motherfucker cools this motherfucker *down*.'

'How come you don't stink if you sweat so much?' asks her friend.

'This motherfucker spray Febreeze. Spray it all the motherfuckin' time!' At this point she produces a can of Febreeze from her handbag, gesturing with it as she speaks. 'Even if the doorbell goes I be sprayin' Febreeze because I be smokin' weed and it could be my motherfuckin' parole officer. No problem. Got my motherfuckin' Febreeze.' She begins spraying Febreeze about the bus. 'Fresh and cool as a motherfucker!'

She continues spraying as a woman across the aisle begins to cough and wave her hand in front of her face.

———

The poor in Las Vegas are among the most bedraggled and wretched in America. Every day I see something that stays with me, something that reminds me that the whole city is one spin of the wheel from total collapse.

Driving home from a friend's house at midnight, I see a procession of two. The man pushes a supermarket trolley full of clothes; the woman follows in a motorised wheelchair. I look again and realise the clothes in the cart are a sleeping child.

One night we catch a bus to the Strip. Opposite us sits a young father with two children. He is high and falling asleep. The kids are filthy, their faces grimy and hair matted. The younger is obviously mentally handicapped. When she accidentally wipes snot on her father he shouts at her and makes everyone uncomfortable. Finally they get off by a golf course in the middle of nowhere. I wonder where they could be going. Later I discover there are drains under the Strip housing a subterranean city of the homeless. One of the entrances is in that area.

Of course, none of this is worse than what you can see on the streets of any big American city, and often not nearly as bad. But in Las Vegas, the city of excess where everything is made grotesque by proximity, these scenes are especially heartbreaking.

Take the Las Vegas buffet. Everyone who visits Vegas, and many locals, will eat at a buffet. In a short time we've been to quite a few. They range across the quality spectrum: from steaming buckets of blancmange and chicken arses to epicurean cornucopias of such extravagance they allow every college boy slob in chinos and reef walkers, or drunk mid-western housewife clutching a plastic guitar full of margaritas the chance to dine, for one night, as a conquering Chinese emperor.

At the better ones the food is superb, mind-boggling in fact: piles of restaurant-quality dishes, including quail, several varieties of crab, sashimi, Beef Wellington with real foie gras, oysters, lobster ravioli, roasted bone marrow, pork rillettes, Sicilian white anchovies, cakes like jewels in the windows at Tiffany's and, at one, honey-glazed pig's tails in little Chinese takeaway containers.

One night we are at one of the best. It is about ten-thirty when the lights start to go out. I am eating blood orange gelato that tastes as if it was flown in that morning from Florence. At the meat station a chef in a white hat dumps a huge tray of Colorado lamb cutlets on the counter. They are close to my favourite food and, even from this distance, and having already consumed four, they look gorgeous.

Suddenly, his station goes dark. Without a pause, the chef picks the tray back up and slides what must be half a sheep into the bin. For a second I can't quite believe what has happened; it's one of those things you're not really equipped to process. I knew there must be waste at a buffet, but this is beyond mere waste: it's like a scene from an ancient chronicle describing the excesses of some monstrous imperial banquet: Cleopatra drinking pearls dissolved in vinegar, or a mad Roman emperor eating larks' tongues out of a slave's crotch. Behind the station I can actually see steam rising out of the bin.

Meanwhile, over by the dessert station, another chef is wrestling with the huge silver vats of gelato. As I take my last mouthful of blood orange, he picks up the vat and, with rubber-gloved hands, starts scraping it into a garbage bag. With its off-pink colour it has uncomfortably flesh-like associations, as if it were liposuction fat being thrown out behind a clinic.

That night we watch a report about poverty in Las Vegas. In it a high school teacher says she discovered students were stealing ketchup packets from the cafeteria so they could make soup for dinner and a girl admits her family has been eating rats.

To point out the inequities and gross contradictions of Las Vegas would be not merely to flirt with cliché but to take it out for a three-star Michelin degustation dinner before returning home to hump it in eighty-two positions. But sometimes even the obvious has to be stated: Las Vegas is American capitalism at its most unrepentantly repulsive. Some days it is enough to make you want to become a card-carrying Communist of the old-school, backs-against-the-wall, blood-in-the-streets, *viva-la-revolución* variety. If I wake up one morning to find Señora SloMo, Alejandro and the tamale lady banging on my door and denouncing me to an angry mob as a class traitor, I can't really say I'd blame them.

Casino owners are big celebrities in Las Vegas. They are always referred to in the press as casino 'moguls', as if they sit around on silk cushions having Persian poetry read to them. They have made their fortunes in Las Vegas, but they don't seem to do much for the place, at least when compared to corporate titans in other American capitals.

Steve Wynn is the owner of the eponymous Wynn Las Vegas. He essentially invented the modern Las Vegas super resort when he opened the Mirage in 1989. He is so tanned and has had so much plastic surgery and Botox he looks like the love child of Valentino and William Shatner. Occasionally he will perform a lordly act of charity: one Christmas he handed out a million dollars' worth of gift vouchers, like Scrooge buying Tiny Tim a turkey. At a museum inside the Bellagio casino, which he also built, he used to display his modern art collection, considered one of the world's finest. But he was really only doing it as a tax write-off and the entrance fee was higher than the Louvre's.

Sheldon Adelson is the owner of the Venetian casino. In 2012 he spent at least $72 million on donations to the failed election campaigns of Newt Gingrich and Mitt Romney. He also created a Jewish school in Vegas but his single biggest act of charity was a donation of $100 million to an organisation that takes Jewish children on trips to Israel. I know what you're thinking: with all the suffering and poverty in the world, at least there's some consolation in knowing that middle-class kids can finally get that holiday they've always wanted.

———

There's a lot of talk in Las Vegas about Zappos, an internet retail company that has bought huge tracts of land Downtown, where it is moving its headquarters. One day I interview the CEO, Tony Hsieh, for an article I am writing. His publicist requests I take a tour of the company headquarters beforehand.

Zappos is one of those funky Silicon Valley outfits where the boss works from a beanbag and people at meetings hold a fairy wand when it's their turn to talk. Among other corporate aims, it likes to 'create a little weirdness', as if you can be 'weird' on purpose. This makes me very apprehensive.

As soon as I set foot inside, my worst fears are confirmed. Seeing me, the receptionist says, 'Yo, dude!' and 'raises the roof'. The other employees are just as bad: their cubicles look like teenage girls' bedrooms, every square inch covered in pictures of their favourite bands, plastic toys and iPhone photos of their friends. As the tour progresses a group start running around and having a water-pistol fight, just to demonstrate how fun-loving they are.

Every time the tour comes to a different section, everyone in that department has to bang a drum, shake a rattle or, most memorably, blow a plastic trumpet. It is weird, but only in the sense that being stuck in a T.G.I. Friday's forever would be weird.

As something of a contrarian, I love telling people I live in Las Vegas. It simultaneously arouses their frustrated carnal instincts and outrages their sense of propriety, as if I had casually mentioned I enjoy drink driving or couldn't be bothered with safe sex. I especially love outraging intellectual types, most especially non-Americans: telling them you live in America makes them recoil in horror; adding that you live in Las Vegas—not *at least*, say, New York— is to invite reactions ranging from scoffing laughter (the assumption being that you must be joking) to gentle head-tilted enquiries as to whether you are doing this to make some kind of ironic statement. It's like saying you live in a sewer, but not in the nice part, in the rat's nest. Or where the rats shit. Or where the rat shit gets washed up in some distant corner of the sewer and gets old and fermented and breeds new diseases and mutant crocodiles.

Still, it is true: Vegas doesn't have much going for it in the high-culture department. The city's citizens are, on average, uneducated and the schools are among the worst in the country. There are a few quirky museums and a new performing arts centre (musicals, mostly) but little else. The visual art scene is pretty sad, mostly comprising of community exhibition spaces and vanity galleries owned by some of the world's greatest exponents of the schools of Sad Clown Expressionism, Showgirl Futurism and Faggoty Sculptures of Art Nouveau Acrobats.

One afternoon I decide to check out the local literary festival. It is a disaster. Admittedly the weather is freezing but that doesn't excuse the fact that the program consists of half-a-dozen guys trying to sell self-published crime and fantasy novels and a few second-hand stores flogging overpriced cookbooks.

There are two stages for readings. On the smaller a woman gets up to talk about her recently published memoir of life as Bing Crosby's niece. The MC introduces her, claps vigorously into the microphone, then sits in the middle of the front row, the only audience member. On the other stage a woman is reading a recipe for a banana cake as a poem to a shivering crowd of five. When we try to walk in we are asked for $10. We go to a casino and get drunk instead.

⁓

The time comes to return to Australia, at least for a little while. As we pack, I realise we have a freezer full of meat and other groceries I don't want to throw away. I try to take them to a neighbour but he's not there, so I cross the road to the black family's home. 'Hello,' I say to one of the little girls playing in the dirt out front. 'Is your mummy home?' She shakes her head. 'What about your daddy?'

She goes inside and reappears with a shirtless man who looks as if he ought to be handcuffed and sitting in a gutter on an episode of *Cops*. Midway through my spiel about not wanting to waste the food, etcetera, I look at the plastic bags and realise they're full of meat from Wholefoods: some of it cost almost $20 a pound, most of the packages are still wrapped with the prices stuck on them.

What does he make of this offer? Does he see me as a condescending white yuppie come to bestow charity upon him? Is he resentful of the fact that I spend this kind of money on steak and organic chicken? Oh, shit: why did I tell him I'm going away? He'll probably come and rob the house the moment we leave.

Looking at the bag he ashes his cigarette, nods and takes it from me. Extending his hand he introduces himself. His name is just a collection of sounds. I get him to repeat it but I still have no better understanding. It occurs to me that he doesn't give a shit where the meat comes from or how much it cost.

As I bid him goodbye he says something else. 'I'm sorry?' I ask.

It sounds like 'wadda-tadda-nadda-dood'.

I can't bring myself to ask him to repeat it again, so I just smile, nod and pretend. 'Ha ha, yes!' I call, heading off back across the street.

It is a while later, on our way to the airport, that I realise what he had said. I am sitting in the back of the cab and my mind is wandering, thinking about Las Vegas, about Australia and home and what that means. After so many years on the road something has changed. I still have itchy feet but can do without the constant state of unknowing: I don't want to wake up anymore with a sudden start of unfamiliarity, don't want to fall asleep in sheets full of strange pubic hair, can live happily knowing I'll never ride another Greyhound. Could home be Las Vegas? Fate, it seemed, had forced us on a blind date. To our mutual surprise, both of us had rather enjoyed it. I guess we'd text a while and go to IKEA before we'd call it forever. It is then that the letters turn on the game show puzzle board, the static washes away and my neighbour's words reveal themselves.

Oh, of course: 'Welcome to the neighbourhood.'

Acknowledgements

Thanks to Colette Vella at MUP for taking on this book, my editor Ali Lavau, and my agent Benython Oldfield. Also thanks to Wil Anderson, Annabel Crabb, Benjamin Law and anybody else who has said—or will say—nice things about my writing. Thanks to Claire Smith for inventing "the Two-Ten factor", to Lee, once more, and to all the people I have met all over the world, most of whom I will never see again but whose oblivious generosity gives this vampire life.

Also by Brendan Shanahan

In Turkey I am Beautiful

'Endlessly observant and curious; real passion underpins his writing.'
—*Sun Herald*

'Full of fascinating anecdotes, rich with warmth, humour and historical anecdotes.'
—*Courier Mail*

Two years after his first visit, travel writer Brendan Shanahan returned to Turkey. After catching up with old friends in Istanbul, he set off on a journey in the country's secretive east where, among other adventures, he found himself in the middle of a gunfight, was propositioned by a gang of teenage boys and swam to Armenia in his underpants. Returning to Istanbul, Brendan agreed to run a friend's carpet shop. With only the dubious help of a loveable but wildly unstable drug addict, the results were occasionally disastrous, frequently hilarious and often poignant.

Available from Melbourne University Publishing
www.mup.com.au

Also by Brendan Shanahan

The Secret Life of the Gold Coast

'An energetic and searching book'
—*The Age*

The Gold Coast: City of the Future; metropolis of dreams. In less than fifty years a tiny holiday town of fibro shacks and mangrove swamps has grown to become a city of almost a million people and an embodiment of our unquenchable lust for surf, sun and sand. Set against a backdrop of marina developments for the near-dead, a rampant drug culture, the underground porn industry and the anarchy of schoolies week, *The Secret Life of the Gold Coast* is a disturbing but often comical expose that trawls the underbelly of Gold Coast life while pondering the elusive nature of Paradise and the unexpected consequences of our desires.

Available from Melbourne University Publishing
www.mup.com.au